T

POWER

of

SMALL

...T THE AUTHORS

LINDA KAPLAN THALER is the CEO and Chief Creative Officer and ROBIN KOVAL is the President of The Kaplan Thaler Group. The company is ranked as one of the fastest-growing advertising agencies in the United States. Kaplan Thaler and Koval are the co-authors of the US bestselling titles *Bang!* and *The Power of Nice* Together they have been featured in *USA Today*, the *New York Times* and *Business Week*. Kaplan Thaler and Koval both live in New York.

www.thepowerofsmallbook.com
www.kaplanthaler.com

The

POWER

of

SMALL

Why Little Things Make All the Difference

LINDA KAPLAN THALER & ROBIN KOVAL

Published in 2011 by Virgin Books, an imprint of Ebury Publishing
A Random House Group Company

2 4 6 8 10 9 7 5 3 1

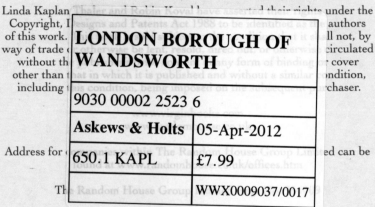

LONDON BOROUGH OF WANDSWORTH

9030 00002 2523 6	
Askews & Holts	05-Apr-2012
650.1 KAPL	£7.99
	WWX0009037/0017

Address for the Random House Group Limited can be
found at www.randomhouse.co.uk/offices.htm

The Random House Group Limited Reg. No. 954009

A CIP catalogue record for this book is available from the British Library

ISBN 9780753539903

Mixed Sources
Product group from well-managed
forests and other controlled sources
www.fsc.org Cert no. TT-COC-002139
© 1996 Forest Stewardship Council

Printed and bound in the UK by
CPI Bookmarque, Croydon, CR0 4TD

For Emily and Michael —
from your first small steps,
you have made my heart leap.
—Linda Kaplan Thaler

For Kenny and Melissa and the belief
in miracles large and small.
—Robin Koval

Contents

. . .

Acknowledgments   ix

Foreword   xiii

Introduction   xv

Chapter 1: The Power of Small   1

Chapter 2: Small Truths   12

Chapter 3: Make Small Talk   24

Chapter 4: Go the Extra Inch   41

Chapter 5: Take Baby Steps   56

Chapter 6: Watch Your Cues and Clues   71

Chapter 7: Little Mistakes Spell Disaster   88

Chapter 8: Make It Big by Thinking Small   108

Chapter 9: Small Changes the World   122

Index   135

Acknowledgments

. . .

There are so many people whose help and guidance have contributed to making *The Power of Small* a reality.

First, our thanks go to Richard Abate at Endeavor, for believing in us from the beginning and for continuing to be our strongest advocate. Richard's tenacity and ingenuity helped us write what we believe is the perfect book for our challenging times.

Our heartfelt thanks go to Tamara Jones, our writing muse and a brilliant journalist. Tamara kept us honest and stuck with us through the long haul. And thanks for the brownies! Thank you to Sandra Bark, for her terrific research acumen, ebullient personality, and unfailing spirit. Even when the task seemed impossible, Sandra worked tirelessly to uncover the facts, quotes, and anecdotes that brought meaning to our ideas.

Thank you to our amazing editor at Doubleday, Roger Scholl, for providing the original inspiration for this work. Roger, you have the uncanny ability to ferret out the diamonds in the rough, to keep us on course and true to our voice—and always with kindness and diplomacy. In addition, we want to thank the many other folks at Doubleday who helped make this book possible: Meredith McGinnis, Michael Palgon, Talia Krohn, Liz Hazelton, and Roger's assistant, Anna Thompson.

A warm thank-you to Karl Turkel for his incredible and charming cover design and for finding the perfect mascot (our "ant") for the book, as well as to Phil McCobb and Paul Kirchner for generously donating their time to give our ant life. And thank you to Creative Directors Alex Spak and Jill Danenberg for all their brilliant advertising ideas. Thanks to Josh Comers for contributing his comedic genius.

Special thanks to our publicist, Mark Fortier, and his assistant, Danny Estremera, who have been instrumental in bringing "The Power of Small" to the world in a very big way. Thank you to Evan Greenberg, Leslie Jacobus, Joe Rella, Brenda Vinton, and Davis Stewart all Allscope Media, for giving us so much of their time, expertise, and media savvy. And thank you to the talented crew at Fat Free, Mike Metz and Dennis Hayes, for designing our website, as well as Kate Noonan and our own Myles Kleeger and Lauren Reilly for helping us navigate the digital world. Thank you to Lisa Bifulco, for producing all our videos with excellence (and always on time and on budget).

A very special word of thanks to our wonderful clients, friends, and co-workers who inspired so many of the stories in our book: Steve Sadove, Dan Amos, Karl Ronn, Patricia Fripp, Scott Fimple, Annamarie Ausnes, Sandie Anderson, Tom Amico, Eric David, Danny Meyer, General Colin Powell, Michelle Alba-Lim, Molly Boren, Dr. Ona Robinson, Amy Sutherland, Anthony Pinizzotto, Edward Davis, Charles Miller III, Kenny Dichter, Tony Hassini, Paul Gumbiner, Greg Davis, Randall Tallerico, Carol Gardner, Sheri Schmelzer, Jen Groover, Warren Brown,

Sandi Genovese, Don Schoendorfer, Greg McHale, Brendan Finn, Dr. Carol Kinsey Goman, Nell Merlino, Adele Horowitz, Syndi Seid, John Breen, Shauna Fleming, Michael Lucco, Greg Lucco, Matthew Greenbaum, and Stu Snodgrass.

Our extra special thanks to comedian extraordinaire Gilbert Gottfried for his wonderful foreword, mega rock legend and marketing guru Gene Simmons, the inspirational and courageous Jamie Clarke, and baseball legend and American icon Yogi Berra, whose wisdom, "I'm not in a slump, I'm just not hitting," got us through some long, difficult nights while struggling to complete the manuscript.

Thank you to Maurice Lévy, the CEO of our parent company, the Publicis Groupe, for your enthusiastic support of all our literary endeavors.

And a resounding thanks to everyone at The Kaplan Thaler Group for their help, guidance, and positive spirit: our tireless assistants, Fran Marzano and Josie Forde; our brilliant Director of Corporate Communications, Tricia Kenney, and the members of her team; Charlotte Lederman for taking on the enormous task of managing all our marketing programs; Erin Creagh; and Charisse Higgins. Thank you to all the other wonderful and supportive executives at KTG: Gerry Killeen, Kevin Sweeney, Greg Davis, and Jeffrey Wolf. And a hearty thank-you to Dennis Marchesiello and all the members of the KTG Graphic Studio for their amazing talents and extraordinary efforts, including John Vila for his keen proofreading skills.

A special thank-you to our families, for their unending support and wonderful stories, which have truly enriched this book:

To my wonderful husband, Fred Thaler, and our children, Emily and Michael, who always keep me honest, and are a constant source of joy and laughter. And to my beloved parents, Bertha and Marvin Kaplan, who have believed in me since day one, and provided such a funny and cautionary tale to the book.

To my beloved husband, Kenny Koval, the man who has been my hero and best friend for nearly three decades. And to the beautiful, talented, and brilliant Melissa Koval: may your future be sprinkled with star dust.

Foreword

. . .

Before we get going here, you probably want to know why I'm writing the foreword to this book. Well, first, I'm a small man. It would have made no sense for Shaquille O'Neal to write it. Second, and let's face it, I'm funnier.

In my line of work, small things make a big difference. If you're a half-beat off, the joke goes over like pork rinds at a bar mitzvah. One off-color comment at a corporate gig, and you'll find yourself on the unemployment line. And that's true in other professions as well. On the other hand, the right one-liner delivered at the right time can solve world hunger and bring peace to the Middle East.

Okay, maybe that's a stretch. But small things really do make an enormous difference. I know. When Robin and Linda's agency created the Aflac Duck, they turned my small talent for quacking into one of the most successful advertising campaigns in history.

Thinking small is even more important in times like these. Let's face it, between global warming, the financial meltdown, and twittering, we don't know what we're facing next. I feel overwhelmed just trying to change a lightbulb. Imagine trying to fix the world. So why not spend a bit more time on the little gestures that can improve our lives and the lives of others? Write a note to thank someone for doing you a favor; tell your kids that you love them;

walk a senior citizen across the street. Then, when we're all foraging for food in the post-apocalyptic economy, that person you held the door for at the pharmacy may share some of their gruel with you.

So read on. Find out why paying attention to the small things can pay major dividends. It's not a long book. Just read one chapter at a time. Or one page at a time. After all, it's the small things that make a difference. Just ask any of my former girlfriends.

Gilbert Gottfried

Introduction

. . .

In a world in which we are urged to see the big picture and grab the brass ring, where the world seems to constantly accelerate with every new website and technological tool, it too often feels as if we don't have the time to sweat the small stuff. The details get lost in a flood of digital data, e-mails, and YouTube videos. We have become a nation of skimmers, our attention limited to sound bites, live video clips, and headlines. Too often, we live our lives as a series of SparkNotes. As a result, the small cues, the simple gestures, the random acts of kindness that give life texture and meaning are too often overlooked or ignored. We feel too pressured to notice the nuances of human behavior, or to bother with the small personal efforts that may, ultimately, win us more attention than our grand acts or intentions. The fact is, no one gets ahead, wins the promotion, or saves the guy or girl, without noticing, sweating over, and taking care of the small stuff.

True, we cannot allow ourselves to become tethered to useless trivia that can overwhelm what is important and prevent us from achieving our goals. We are huge fans of the bestseller *Don't Sweat the Small Stuff*. But at heart Richard Carlson was arguing something different—that in terms of our life journey, we often get caught up in things that really *aren't* all that important, blowing them out of proportion. He focuses more on our spiritual and psychological well-being. What we are arguing is that a lot of "small stuff" at work, and in our personal lives, gets overlooked, or is brushed aside, when it shouldn't be, because it really *does* matter. Taking the time to give a compliment, or being attuned to a colleague or customer's subtle body cues, are not inconsequential actions. They tell a story. They are the details that make or break a relationship, or crack the case, for all you James Patterson or *Law & Order* junkies. It is our small behaviors that so often define us and create an imprint of who we are.

The response to our previous book, *The Power of Nice*, has been overwhelming. Of the countless people who wrote in about the positive power of nice in their lives, from smiling at a cranky co-worker to giving up their bus seat to a stranger, the stories all shared one common thread: the biggest rewards were almost always rooted in the smallest gestures. Yet in our desperate attempt to navigate through the dense forest of endless stimuli, we often forget to notice the trees—or, more important, the leaves on the trees. But it is in those leaves, in their tiny, almost imperceptible shadings, shapes, and scents, that we discover what is real, what is beautiful, and what has meaning.

Believing that it is the small things that make the greatest difference is not just an ideology—it is also timely and pragmatic advice born out of the economically challenged world we live in. Saving for the future is a daunting task, but saving penny by penny is easily done. And it offers rich rewards to those willing to think small. It is a philosophy that can help people reach even the most daunting goals. And if President Obama's presidential campaign has taught us anything, it's that there are no limits to how far each of us can go. We just need to be willing to walk a little bit farther, reach a little bit higher, day after day.

In writing *The Power of Small*, our own lives have been enriched in ways we could never have imagined. We began to notice firsthand how our smallest actions had a positive impact on our business and personal relationships. We became more sensitive to giving praise for a job well done, to taking the extra five minutes to go that extra step, to making that extra call or effort, to adding a simple "I love you" at the end of a phone call with a partner or spouse. We hope this book enriches your life as well, and encourages you to appreciate every wondrous moment of it.

Linda and Robin

THE POWER OF
SMALL

Chapter 1
The Power of Small

We can do no great things—only small things with great love.
—Mother Teresa

Larry was a computer programmer in the sales division of a major San Francisco apparel company. He was the guy who dealt with the data, fixed people's computer problems, and spent long hours creating new ways to slice and dice the numbers. In short, Larry was a self-proclaimed computer nerd.

He would watch the men and women of the sales department and admire their outgoing natures, their easy conversational skills, the way they looked so sophisticated and stylish. Larry often thought to himself, "I can do that. I want to do that." But he had no idea how to go about changing his career path, and he wasn't sure he had the confidence to try. Should he quit his job and go to business school? Should he work nights getting sales experience at a smaller company? Did he need a career coach? He didn't know where to begin. The idea of changing the direction of his life seemed daunting.

Then one day, he strolled into Patricia Fripp's men's hair

salon. Patricia was a pioneer in her field, one of the first to coax men out of utilitarian barbershops and into hip salons. Patricia approached her job with a unique zeal and passion. She strove to give every client a haircut that would say something special about him. Often she changed only the slightest detail—the angle of the part or the length of the sideburns—but she was a master. She sat Larry down in her chair and went to work.

Larry emerged a half hour later with a new look. He showed up at work and all the women cooed, "Larr-y! You look great." At home that night his wife said, "Hon-ey, you look so handsome." Even the young woman at the corner deli where Larry bought his coffee each morning noticed, saying "Mr. L., there's something different about you."

Larry's new haircut and the way it changed his self-perception started a chain reaction within him. It dawned on him that taking even small steps could have a real impact on his life. He bought some new clothes. He started going to the gym more often. He made an effort to smile more. Once he began to think of himself in a different light, others saw him differently as well. When he became friendly with some of the sales managers at work, he confided his desire to switch careers. Soon the head of the sales department offered him a junior position.

Larry not only rose to the challenge, he became the best performer the department ever had. They cut the size of his territory five times and he still outsold everyone else. Before long he was the chief sales executive of the company.

It's obvious that Larry had a natural talent for the business, and he put a lot of hard work into understanding every detail about the merchandise and his customers. His computer wizardry with a spreadsheet didn't hurt, either. But if you ask Larry what changed his life, he'll smile and say that truth be told, he owes his success to one great haircut.

That is the surprising power of our small actions, our subtle shifts in thinking, and our dogged attention to the everyday details in life: They can change everything—our careers, relationships, well-being, and, ultimately, how we impact the world around us.

For Larry, that small transformation became a catalyst for change. Before that haircut, he lacked confidence and direction. He yearned for something different in his life, but didn't know how to create it. He was stuck waiting for something BIG to come along.

The haircut didn't just change how Larry looked; it changed his outlook. Instead of brushing off those early compliments as mere conversational niceties, he took them to heart, and built on them. It was a small beginning, but a genuine one, and for so many of us, that's the most difficult part: taking those first small steps that ultimately lead to a huge difference in our lives.

Small, seemingly insignificant acts are powerful agents of change and growth—if we pay attention to them. Unfortunately, we live in a world where we are constantly told to concentrate on the big things, to not sweat the small stuff. Because of that, we often feel that incremental change doesn't count for much—it doesn't pay off. We celebrate milestones, and ignore the daily victories that herald persistent substantial change over time. As Canadian explorer

Jamie Clarke, who reached the summit of Mount Everest step by careful step, puts it: "There's not only power in small, but magic, too."

That crucial message often gets buried in the minutiae of our everyday lives. So we screen, filter out, and gloss over insignificant, trifling details in order to navigate the hectic world in which we live. And there is some wisdom and value in that: We need to ignore a lot of the "noise" to get on with our lives. Let's face it, if we worry about memorizing all the channels on our cable system, or all the arcane instructions from the Microsoft Word operating manual, we'll never get out of the house each morning.

However, in the process of ignoring the utterly useless and insignificant, we have given short shrift to something that is extraordinarily essential—the small gestures, words, and daily kindnesses that speak volumes about our attention to detail, and our commitment and concern to effect change and make a difference. Checking—or not checking—that e-mail again before sending it out says a lot about how careful and meticulous we would be on a larger project. Taking the time to jot a thank-you note to your son's fourth-grade room mother will make a bigger impression than the designer cupcakes you're bringing for the class party. These are the minor details on which careers, relationships, even lives, often pivot.

We often labor over creating long-term life and career goals and planning strategies to accomplish them. But life rarely works according to such a grand design. Sometimes, the small, spontaneous acts make all the difference. That can be especially true in matters of the heart.

A Little Bit of Kindness

Simone and Jake had been dating for nearly two years. In Simone's mind, they were a perfect couple. She was convinced that Jake was the man she wanted to marry. Jake, on the other hand, wasn't ready to make a formal commitment. Every time Simone tried to talk to him about their future, he would change the subject.

As time passed, Simone began to despair. Finally, she decided that she had to take a stand. If he didn't get serious about their relationship, she would have to break up with him. Simone knew that it would devastate her to walk away from Jake, but she saw no other option. She certainly wasn't going to beg him to propose.

One evening, as Simone and Jake were hurrying along the street to dinner, they passed a homeless man, huddled against the icy wind. Simone, who had been wrapped up in her concerns, stopped in her tracks, jarred back to reality by the sight of this cold, dirty, hungry stranger.

"I'll be right back," she told Jake.

Simone dashed across the street toward an open thrift store; next, she went into the deli on the corner. When she returned, her arms were full. Simone walked over to the man sitting on the street. In the larger bag was a big woolen coat. The smaller bag held a container of hot soup and a freshly made sandwich.

"Here," she said simply. "This is for you."

As Jake and Simone walked on to the restaurant, Simone silently vowed to tell Jake that night how she felt.

Once seated, she took a deep breath. "Jake," she began, "I have something to tell you."

"I have to tell you something first," he interrupted. And then he leaned over and blurted out, "I don't have a ring, Simone, I'm sorry. But I have to ask you: Will you marry me?"

Simone was overwhelmed. "Why now?" she managed to stammer.

"When I saw you stop to give that homeless man a coat and a warm meal," Jake said, "I thought, 'How could I not spend the rest of my life with someone this kind?'"

Needless to say, Simone said yes. Today, Simone and Jake are happily married, and the proud parents of three wonderful children.

Simone's reaction to the homeless man wasn't premeditated. It was a small, spur-of-the-moment action, and yet it had gigantic repercussions. Her instinctive act of kindness struck Jake like a lightning bolt—everything he needed to know about the next twenty years of his life was right in front of him. With that one act, he learned more about Simone than a thousand conversations could have told him.

"Most couples in trouble think that for things to improve, extraordinary changes, if not a miracle, have to take place," says Howard Markman, a professor of psychology at the University of Denver. Couples have a tendency to think that it's the other person that needs to change. But we can't change other people—all we can control is what we do.

"The breakthrough," says Professor Markman, "comes when we realize that by making even small changes in ourselves, we can effect big, positive changes."

Simone had just naturally done something to help another human being in need—offering him a ten-dollar thrift-shop coat and a two-dollar cup of soup—and the course of her entire life changed. These are the kinds of changes that can take place in our lives and the lives of those around us when we unleash the power of small.

And the way to do that is to learn to pay attention to the right details.

No one better grasps the importance of small details than John Wooden, the first man to make it to the Basketball Hall of Fame as both a player and a coach. In his book, *A Lifetime of Observations and Reflections On and Off the Court*, Wooden points out that seemingly innocuous things make the difference between "champions and near-champions." He would begin the first squad meeting of a new season with the same demonstration, year after year. The demonstration wasn't about showing his college players how to execute the perfect dunk or fast break: What the legendary coach wanted to teach them was how to put on their socks.

"I wanted absolutely no folds, wrinkles, or creases of any kind on the sock," he explains. "I would demonstrate for the players and then have the players demonstrate for me. This may seem like a nuisance . . . but I had a very practical reason for being meticulous about this. Wrinkles, folds, and creases can cause blisters. Blisters interfere with performance during practice and games . . . These seemingly trivial matters, taken together and added to many, many other so-called trivial matters, build into something very big: namely, your success."

In the business world, that kind of attention to detail is

exactly what we need to both avoid missteps and perfect our own winning jump shots. When we launched The Kaplan Thaler Group, we didn't envision becoming an agency with a billion dollars in billings that would be acquired by a public company. We didn't have a five-year or ten-year goal—we had twenty thousand little goals, because we have found that when you focus on solving the myriad problems of today, you create the most promising tomorrow. But to do that, you need an environment where, no matter how small the task, everyone is willing to pitch in.

We began as a six-person operation and grew to fifteen before we even had enough chairs to go around in the cramped brownstone attic that served as our corporate headquarters. Although we served different functions at the agency, we had an egalitarian attitude toward daily responsibilities and chores. Each of us had to carry a bag of trash out every night and surreptitiously toss it in the school Dumpster across the street, because we couldn't afford our own. And while we can laugh sheepishly now at stealth garbage duty, that daily task convinced us that we had the team we needed to grow our business—employees who were both flexible and loyal. Everyone understood that no job was too small. It's easier to complain than comply when it comes to getting the little things done. But our bosses, our colleagues, and even our friends learn a lot about us by the way we handle the smallest tasks, the briefest encounters, the tiniest details.

Linda recalls that when she went on her very first date with her husband, Fred, it was one small action that convinced her he was the one. "It was a particularly chilly night, and I was about to walk out the door with my coat only halfway buttoned. Without saying a word, Fred reached over and buttoned up the rest of my coat. It may have been cold out, but that one action melted my heart. Twenty-two years later, Fred still checks to make sure our coats are buttoned, whether it's mine or the kids'."

Girl Talk

A few years back, the Girl Scouts asked us to create a campaign that would encourage girls to remain involved in math and science when they entered their tween years. Research has revealed that although girls outshine boys in those academic arenas when they are in elementary school, they suddenly seem to lose confidence in math and science when they enter middle school. The parents we spoke to in our research groups were baffled. They believed they were doing everything possible to fuel their young daughters' curiosity about and passion for these subjects. After three exhausting days of focus groups, one mother casually mentioned that she wanted to record a science show for her daughter, but because her husband was out of town, she was unable to do so. Our ears perked up. "Why did you say that?" we asked.

"Well, as I told my daughter, I'm not really good with all that technology stuff. I think it's like a girl thing or something," she chuckled. For us, the lightbulb went on when we heard this mother's remark. Her casual words led us to write an award-winning commercial underscoring the importance of mothers not only encouraging their daughters' natural curiosity in math and science, but being more aware of the subtle cues that reveal their own insecurities and negative predispositions. In essence, women had been inadvertently passing on the "girls can't do math or science" myth without even being consciously aware of it. That campaign went on to win the White House Project Award for building self-esteem among young women.

In advertising, an obsession for detail is essential in creating an effective ad, because every second counts. A Hollywood director can tell his story over two and a half hours, on a twenty-foot silver screen, to a dedicated audience sitting in a dark room paying full attention. In advertising, we must compress our message into fifteen or thirty seconds that flash across a TV screen most likely playing in the background of busy multitasking families. Every nuance, every syllable needs to continually draw you in, or you'll mute, fast-forward, or flip to another channel. The rule of thumb is that if an ad doesn't capture a viewer's attention within the first five seconds, you're history. And the subject matter deals with small, everyday problems that certainly wouldn't be blockbuster fare—"What should I make my family for dinner?" "How do I stop my hair from frizzing in the rain?" "Where can I get a pair of jeans that will make my butt look smaller?" Our success, therefore, is measured in how artfully we portray the moment the ferret peers out from a BabyBjörn in a Kraft Bagel-fuls commercial, or perfecting just the right notes that make the Toys "R" Us song so memorable that millions of Americans can still sing it by heart.

But what about the power of small in our personal and professional lives?

We all want to change or improve our lives and advance our careers. In fact, each January, many of us make a list of life-changing resolutions that we forget by Valentine's Day. Every Monday, we focus our attention on winning that big brass ring, or corner office, or the big promotion, instead of *doing* the small things every day that will get us there. The secret to getting ahead in life sometimes involves changing our perspective from the grandiose and the difficult to the small and doable. Those are the actions that produce tangible results.

Our "small" outlook on life not only drives our business but is present in everything we do—in the way we interact with our employees, our clients, our friends, our family, and, frankly, the random people we encounter each day. The positive impressions we make through little words, deeds, and gestures are what lay the groundwork for success in life. It isn't difficult, but it does take commitment.

In the following chapters we will look at how the power of small, of focusing on the trees as well as the forest, works in various aspects of our lives—and how to make it work for you.

Chapter

Small Truths

> You can gain more control over your life by paying closer attention to the little things.
> —Emily Dickinson

Truth #1: It's a Byte-Size World

The digital age, like it or not, has condensed planet Earth into a cozy community of six billion citizens, and it's shrinking by the nanosecond. Today our neighborhoods have transcended all physical boundaries, as we console each other in chat rooms, blather in blogospheres, and are probably more likely to be in constant contact with a friend who lives across the country than one across the street. We're LinkedIn, YouTubed, Twittered, Facebooked, BlackBerry-ed and Googled at all hours of the day and night. From spanning the globe to find our soul mate (mailorderhusbands.net), to hiring a personal assistant in India for as little as seven dollars an hour (taskseveryday. com), the power to improve our lives, and livelihoods, is but a keystroke away.

We put the small planet effect to good use at The Kaplan Thaler Group, saving millions of dollars in time and money. When we decided to deepen our digital advertising capabilities, for example, we took on a select group of Internet-savvy employees and outsourced our myriad flash design and coding projects as far away as Costa Rica and Mumbai, saving time and money for our clients in the process. In advertising, we often create "animatics"—cartoon versions of a TV spot—so clients can test our commercial ideas before they are produced live on film. Executing those prototype ads used to take two to three weeks, precious time that delays a campaign from airing, and ultimately selling product. But Ezra Krausz, the founder of Animated Storyboard, found an ingenious way to make time disappear. With studios set up in New York, Tel Aviv, and Bangkok, projects essentially follow the sun, with work flowing from one international team to the next, as the day ends in one time zone and dawns in another. By using Ezra's company, we look like heroes to our clients by having a very realistic test commercial produced virtually overnight!

But a byte-sized world also means we are all but a click away from being totally visible and vulnerable to virtually everyone else on the planet. Every website visit and purchase we make is shockingly transparent. Every e-mail can end up making front-page news, as one law firm we know of learned firsthand. The law firm had a partner who repeatedly berated his staff via e-mail. In fact, he once ranted that their performance was so shoddy he was shocked they still had any clients. A week later the partner fired one of the lawyers, who happily e-mailed the partner's abusive notes to their local newspaper! Needless to say, all their clients read it, and it nearly put the firm out of business.

Forget about swimming in a cyber fishbowl—we're paramecia prancing under a microscope, all dressed in see-through shirts. Did you forget to stop at the light? You may be outed at runaredlight.com. Is your yard an overgrown eyesore? Check out the photographic evidence the busybody down the block posted on rottenneighbor.com. Even a news brief in a local paper can ignite a controversy and launch a YouTube crusade. When a teacher in Florida had kindergartners vote on whether or not to banish a disruptive classmate, it wasn't just brought to the attention of the principal or the PTA to resolve: Thousands of Internet petitions demanding the teacher's dismissal immediately bombarded the school district from around the world.

In fact, one of the most notorious outlaws in our ultra-visible new world happens to be a young South Korean woman who, thanks to the Internet, will forever be known as Dog Poop Girl. When the woman's lapdog relieved itself on the floor of a subway train in South Korea, other passengers urged the owner to clean it up, and even offered tissues. The woman refused and said something rude, then got off the train, leaving the mess behind. But another passenger had photographed the incident and posted the pictures on a popular Korean blog. Within hours, the dog owner was the subject of national ridicule. Her identity and personal details about her past were posted, and she was recognized and jeered in public. Soon, media outlets around the world were reporting the story of Dog Poop Girl. The public humiliation reportedly forced Dog Poop Girl to drop out of her university, and post an online warning that further harassment might drive her to suicide.

Our point? Today, all the world really *is* a stage, empowering each of us to steal the spotlight. But it's our performance that will ultimately determine our fate. Be observant of the small things that potentially can make or break your "performance." Train yourself to use the zoom lens in your career and private life. Whether you're in charge of a $10 million operating budget or just the annual family reunion, don't overlook that one item that seems almost too trivial to worry about. Your ability to pay attention to the smallest details can set you apart from your competitors; overlooking it can leave you in their dust.

Truth #2: Small Acts Tell a Larger Story

When Linda first decided to open The Kaplan Thaler Group, she had one piece of Clairol's hair care business— Herbal Essences Shampoo, which she naively thought she could run from her Manhattan brownstone. Steve Sadove, her sole client and then-president of Clairol, tactfully suggested that Linda would at least need a business partner, since her expertise was in the creative side of advertising. Considering she had never run a company, or earned a business degree, Linda reluctantly agreed. Flipping through her Rolodex, she went on a frenzied search for the perfect partner. She wanted someone brilliant, assertive, collaborative, and challenging. The last person she was looking for was a "yes" woman. She instinctively knew she needed someone with the moxie to tell her if the work was veering off track, or if her genius campaign idea would send a client's company into Chapter 11. She needed to hire an alter ego.

After watching Linda eliminate more prospects than an *American Idol* audition, Steve stepped in again. He urged Linda to contact Robin Koval, who handled a number of other Clairol accounts at a large New York ad agency. Linda arranged to meet Robin at Michael's Muffins, a neighborhood coffee shop whose Formica decor was, to put it kindly, a far cry from the power-breakfast venues where Madison Avenue movers and shakers usually ordered their egg whites. Robin was intrigued. As fate would have it, she was also a tad hungry.

When Linda walked in, there sat Robin at one of the wobbly tables with a giant bran muffin in front of her. The muffin had been perfectly sliced in two. She promptly introduced herself: "Hi, I'm Robin Koval. It's great to meet you. I ordered a bran muffin, and it was huge, so I thought we might share it. Of course, if you want your own muffin, or a different kind, I'll just save this for later."

It was business-partner love at first bite. Linda realized that this simple gesture revealed more about Robin than a résumé or references ever could. She had shown herself to be proactive, frugal, collaborative, and willing to take the initiative, even if the task was ordering breakfast. Within an hour, a partnership was taking root.

Eleven years and two hundred employees later, The Kaplan Thaler Group remains the only agency of its size in America founded and run by women and is consistently ranked as one of the fastest-growing agencies in the country. Getting there wasn't a piece of cake. But it started with half a muffin.

You can learn so much from the small details in life. Does an interviewee look you in the eye, or does he or she look away, signaling a sense of insecurity or a lack of interest? How many business relationships and personal relationships get off on the wrong foot because of a missed cue or lost moment?

Marriage counselors will tell you that the rolling of a spouse's eye in the course of a therapy session can signal an impending divorce long before an attorney is hired; that one reflexive action often comes from a deep well of contempt and resentment. Analysts and pollsters know too well that voters don't remember the big issues in political debates; it is the smaller moments, like a candidate's sneering retort or witty one-liner that is often the turning point. And if you really want to learn about a prospective employer, hours of Googling may not reveal what a few minutes in the reception area will. Arrive five or ten minutes early, and just drink in the atmosphere. Are people sequestered in their offices behind closed doors, or wandering in and out, talking to each other? When the phone rings, what kind of corporate image does the receptionist convey—cold and haughty, or casual and friendly? Doing online research beforehand is a great idea, of course, but don't stop there. Your eyes, your ears, and your intuition can yield something no search engine can dig up: the subtle signs that speak to a company's culture and atmosphere.

Truth #3: Everyone Matters

Linda remembers calling her mother, who lives in West Palm Beach, the night of the 2000 presidential election to tell her that Florida, which at first seemed to have gone to Al Gore, suddenly had been declared for George Bush:

"Well, Linda, I'm not surprised that there is confusion about the results, considering how hard it was to read those ballots," my mother said. "Your dad thinks he voted for Pat Buchanan!"

"How is that possible?" I asked. (My father had always been a staunch Democrat.)

"It's possible because the punch holes were so close together; it was easy to make a mistake," my mother explained. "And I think several other folks in our condo made the same error."

I dismissed my mother's concerns with a breezy reassurance: "Well, I wouldn't worry about it. After all, a couple of hundred retirees in Palm Beach County are certainly not going to decide our next president."

The rest is for the history books. But the ballot battle that ended up in the Supreme Court all started with one small problem, and one person's misconceived solution. Theresa LePore, the former supervisor of elections for Palm Beach County, designed the famous "butterfly ballot" to accommodate the long list of candidates' names and supposedly make them easier to read. Instead, the confusing piece of cardboard led to thousands of miscounted and lost votes. Changing the design arguably ignited the series of events that ultimately determined the presidency, and the course of history. The ripple effect of small actions can never be underestimated.

It's easy to dismiss the potential impact of a single individual or employee, until you realize that one voice from even the most unexpected quarter can solve an ongoing business problem, galvanize a community, or change the world.

Several years back a major restaurant chain that was a former client of ours was losing a ton of money because its crystal was breaking with alarming frequency. Regional and district managers met at one of the restaurants to discuss what to do. Should they devise a new training program for the waitstaff? Replace all glassware with a different brand? A busboy, overhearing the discussion, pulled one of the executives aside and took him to the kitchen. There, he demonstrated how the commercial dishwashers the restaurant had installed would vibrate. Repeated exposure to those vibrations, he suggested, might have weakened and ultimately shattered the crystal. The dishwashers were replaced, and the breakage stopped, saving the company millions of dollars in the years ahead, and earning the busboy a $150,000 tip.

Corporate research shows that the humble, old-fashioned employee suggestion box can be one of the most effective money savers—and moneymakers—a company of any size can have. The Chicago-based National Association of Suggestion Systems estimates that employee suggestion programs have saved organizations more than $2 billion. Moreover, 37 percent of the suggestions employees submit are adopted. Among them was the idea a janitor came up with when the historic El Cortez Hotel in San Diego decided to install an additional elevator to better serve its guests. Engineers had drawn up plans that would require closing the hotel for several months so that a shaft could be cut through each floor of the hotel. A janitor concerned about the mess this would create, as well as the jobs lost while the hotel was closed, offered a suggestion that was both tidy and inspired. Why not build the elevator on the outside of the hotel? This way the hotel could avoid the loss of revenue due to closing and spare employee layoffs, and no guests would be inconvenienced, since the construction would take place on the exterior of the building. The engineers agreed and the El Cortez became the first hotel to give visitors a bird's-eye view of beautiful San Diego Bay as they ascend to their rooms. Today, outside elevators are an admired mainstay of some of the world's poshest resorts.

Truth #4: A Little Good Goes a Long Way

Ten years ago, Scott Fimple was a naval petty officer in Washington, D.C. On shore duty, he worked in a large office building with a confusing labyrinth of floors and wings.

One morning, Scott was walking through the lobby on his way to lunch when he spotted an older man in a civilian suit. He looked like he was lost.

Scott approached the visitor with a smile. "Can I help you?" he asked.

By coincidence, the gentleman turned out to be on his way to meet with Scott's superior officer. Scott introduced himself and escorted the man to his boss's office. They then exchanged pleasantries and went their separate ways.

Later that year, Scott's superior officer summoned him with good news: After years of stellar service, Scott was being awarded a highly coveted Navy Commendation Medal. Overwhelmed, Scott stammered out his thanks.

It was only later that he learned that his award was the result of a letter of recommendation from Admiral Dwayne Griffith, who oversaw every department in Scott's building. Scott was mystified: He had never actually met Admiral Griffith. Why would he personally put Scott up for such an honor?

Turns out that the "stranger" to whom Scott had shown a much appreciated courtesy when he escorted him to his captain's office a few months earlier was none other than the admiral himself, dressed in civilian clothes for an off-duty lunch with a friend.

Nothing terrible would have happened to Scott Fimple if he hadn't offered to help the admiral, and the man obviously would have found his way to the right office. The point is that it wasn't Scott's job to escort him, and in fact, there was no expectation that he should. But Scott made a random decision to do what felt right. What is interesting is what *not* making that choice might have cost him! That is the real moral of this story: When you do nothing, you are doing something. You are closing the door to an opportunity. Every interaction we have should be viewed as a door that has the potential to lead you to a different place. In the business world, our grand plans, at times, need to be dismantled and broken down into the smallest actions. Every phone call, every e-mail, every point of contact with a customer, client, patient, or colleague is an opportunity to excel, to do the unexpected, and in doing so, reveal yourself.

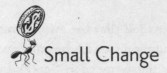

Small Change

BECOME A MINI-TASKER. Do you find that the things on your to-do list never seem to get crossed off, but just get carried from day to day, for weeks at a time? That's because "sell the house" or finish that major research or marketing project is a tall order. Instead of making a list of big, difficult-to-achieve goals at the beginning of your workweek, create an "action list" and reenvision those goals into "mini-tasks" you can actually accomplish on a day-to-day basis. Instead of writing down "sell the house," create a series of smaller steps: Call the broker. (Check.) Write a listing for the house. (Check.) Hire a repair person to fix that broken basement window. (Check.) Instead of panicking over the big things that haven't been done, relish the satisfaction from smaller accomplishments that lead to the overall goal.

APPRECIATE THE LITTLE THINGS. Traffic was a nightmare, your new client was late to the meeting and set your day back by half an hour. And even lunch had its mishaps, unless mustard vinaigrette on a white blouse has become a hot fashion statement. Okay, hit the "pause" button. Take a breath and give yourself a few moments to tally up the things that went right today. Did your son call you to thank you for helping him with his school science project? Did your boss compliment a member of your team? Make a list of five positive things that happened in the course of a stressful day. Appreciate them. Reflect on what you did to make those things happen. Try to do more of those things tomorrow.

MAKE SMALL IMPRESSIONS. It's hard to wow them every day. And let's face it, we live in a society where the question is often "What have you done for me lately?" So look for ways to insert a positive impression, no matter how small, into every encounter. Start every meeting with a compliment for the most junior individual in the room. Bring extra treats and baggies to the dog park. Be the person who hits the elevator "Hold" button for the straggler in the lobby. Keep an extra umbrella in your office. These little, positive acts take virtually no effort, but they compound over time to create an overall impression of you as a "go to" person. And when you need to call in a favor, you'll be repaid with interest.

Chapter 3

Make Small Talk

I can live for two months on a good compliment.
—Mark Twain

A few years ago, a woman told us a story of two families who lived through the terror of Nazi Germany. The names had faded from her memory, so we'll call them the Muellers and the Schmidts.

Two shoemakers had their shops directly across the street from each other in a small German village outside of Berlin. It was the early 1930s, and the Nazi regime was just beginning to take power. Like clockwork, the two men would arrive promptly at 8 a.m. to open their shops so each wouldn't risk losing customers to the other if one shop was closed.

Yet every morning, as Saul Mueller unlocked the front door to his store, he would pause to tip his hat, nod his head, and say, "Hello, Herr Schmidt!" to his biggest competitor. Hans Schmidt would reply in kind with a polite "Hello, Herr Mueller!" from across the street.

One morning, Saul's youngest daughter, Anna, accompanied him to work. After hearing her father's warm salutation to his archrival, she looked up at him and wondered aloud, "Papa, why do you say hello to that man? He's not your friend."

Saul replied, "Dear Anna, as Jews we are taught that you must always greet your neighbor with a few friendly words. Even if that neighbor is your competitor."

As Hitler's grotesque vise tightened around Europe, much changed in the shoemakers' village. As his day-to-day life became more restricted, Saul glimpsed Hans less frequently, but he never failed to greet him with a proper hello whenever he did. One morning, in the predawn darkness, Saul and his family were awakened by the sound of men pounding on their front door. The German army was rounding up all of the Jews for deportation to Auschwitz. As daylight broke, Saul and his family stood shivering and scared in the town square along with several other Jewish families. Suddenly, he heard a voice call to him from down the street.

"Good morning, Herr Mueller!" Hans cried out.

"Good morning, Herr Schmidt," Saul automatically replied.

Hans, seeing the tragic scene before him, and realizing what was about to happen, thought quickly and rushed over to the guards. "You cannot arrest this family," he protested. "They are not Jewish."

The guard shot him a menacing look. "And how do you know that, Herr Schmidt?"

"Because he is my cousin, that's how I know."

Hans's authoritative demeanor and unwavering tone convinced the soldiers that he must be telling the truth. They let the Mueller family go.

The two rival shoemakers never saw each other again. The Muellers fled to France, and then to England. They finally settled in the United States, where they lived very long, full lives, raising their children, and living to see their grandchildren and several great-grandchildren. Because of a simple greeting each morning, just that slight effort to reach out to another human being and acknowledge the bonds between them, the Mueller family was saved.

There is nothing small about small talk.

Starved for Conversation

Sadly, we are so pressed for time in today's world that we routinely dismiss casual conversation as idle chitchat, a waste of time and energy. Too many of us pass up opportunities to exchange pleasantries with our own children, let alone with the neighbor down the street. In a society where the average family moves every five years, we seem to place less and less value on catching up with the couple next door: How was the trip to Yellowstone? What's new at work? Is your daughter still playing tennis? Shooting the breeze is seen as a waste of time.

The era of the Internet and e-mail has further compounded this tendency to retreat into silence, transforming our daily conversations into sterile, digitized bytes that stream anonymously across the Web. As Studs Terkel said, "We are more and more into communications and less and less into communication." How many times during the workday do you "speak" with a co-worker down the hall via e-mail? How often are our communications delivered by Outlook, rather than in person or by phone? How much poorer are our interactions when tone of voice, facial and hand gestures, and body language are cut out of the equation? Dr. Lester Lefton, a behavioral psychologist and president of Kent State University, tells us that "in a day when everyone is communicating by BlackBerry and IM, or telecommuting from home in sweatpants all day instead of interacting with colleagues face to face, the art of social interaction is clearly diminished. We lose some of that nuanced social skill." To be sure, MySpace, Facebook, and LinkedIn have given us a wealth of "friends" with whom we will never have a real-time, face-to-face conversation. The *New York Times* recently describing visiting MySpace and Facebook profiles as "an endless cocktail party where everybody shows up at a different time and slaps a yellow Post-it note on the refrigerator."

The result? We are losing the human texture in even our simplest conversations. We are becoming more and more cut off from human interaction, from the chance encounters and casual acquaintances that have, until recently, made up a part of our lives and at times changed their course. Our conversations have become very directed and informational. We have become, as psychologist Bernardo Carducci points out, an incredibly shy culture. Not surprisingly, social phobia, according to the American Psychological Association, has become the third most common mental illness in America, affecting 13 percent of the population.

When we "cut the small talk" with others, we drive a wedge between human interactions. As Carducci remarks, "the purpose of small talk is to get everything started. Every great love story, every major business deal, involves that initial contact." Small talk is the social lubricant that brings people together, regardless of their differences. And we can profit from the experience in surprising ways.

Charlie's Angel

Charlie was an African-American auto mechanic who worked at a Ford dealership in Detroit in the early 1970s. The bay where he changed oil was the first one people passed in the shop. Everyone who passed by was greeted with an infectious smile and a warm hello. Charlie had the gift of gab and, not surprisingly, attracted a slew of loyal customers.

One of Charlie's regulars was Bill, a wealthy white businessman who loved to shoot the breeze with the gregarious mechanic while Charlie worked on his car. Often the whole shop would hear the two chuckling over some silly joke or outlandish story. During an era marked by racial turbulence and distrust, small talk was the thread that connected their lives, black and white, rich and poor.

One day, Charlie had a surprising visit from a rather well-dressed gentleman. Bill had passed away, and the stranger turned out to be the attorney representing Bill's estate. The attorney announced that Bill had left something for Charlie in his will: the deed to a profitable hardware store in downtown Detroit. Dumbfounded, Charlie wondered why Bill would do such a thing. They were, after all, only casual acquaintances. The answer was simple: Bill believed in him. His color-blind camaraderie with Charlie, and the warmth of their banter over the years, had revealed more about the mechanic's character to Bill than any sociological treatise on race relations.

Bill was right about Charlie. The windfall he inherited didn't change who he was one bit. He wasn't really cut out to be a hardware store owner, so he sold the business. Spending sprees weren't Charlie's style either, and the only outward sign of his newfound wealth was the brand-new green Ford LTD he bought and proudly drove to work each day. The money also allowed him to fulfill his fantasy of taking his wife to New York City and staying in style at the fabled Waldorf Astoria. In fact, the couple became regulars there. But by 8 o'clock Monday morning, Charlie would be back at work at the dealership, fixing other people's cars and making new friends. He stayed until the day the dealership closed down. The last time a co-worker saw Charlie, he was sitting on an island in the Detroit River, fishing. He looked happy.

Our point? Charlie never had a "plan" in mind when he engaged in his brief conversations with Bill, but because of his willingness, his eagerness to reach out to others and take an interest in their lives, one of those encounters helped Charlie to fulfill a dream, a dream that might otherwise have never been realized.

Small talk allows people to discover common ground by gently exploring one another's interests, passions, and opinions. For example, at Kaplan Thaler, we often find our best clues to what a client may like or dislike during the small talk before we sit down to a formal meeting. Finding common ground usually takes a matter of seconds, but the groundwork it lays down can last the life of a relationship. Both of us were nervous about how to break the ice with a gruff new client the afternoon he arrived for an initial meeting at our agency. With Linda trying to wrap up a phone call with another client, it was up to Robin to hold down the fort with our taciturn visitor. She discovered he had grown up in Massachusetts. Robin mentioned that her husband, Kenny, had spent childhood summers at a beloved summer camp there and mentioned that they were hoping to buy a vacation home around that same lake. The gruff client lit up. He not only knew the lake, but he loved it as well, and owned waterfront property there. By the time the actual business meeting began, Robin had a potential lead for her real-estate dreams, and we had a much more relaxed, friendlier client in our important meeting. Small talk helps us discover ways to connect that might otherwise remain hidden, and allows us to avoid the land mines that can destroy a relationship down the line. It allows the delicate threads of disparate lives to intertwine. In today's wired world, most of us limit our small talk, at best, to those we already know, or those we feel can help us professionally or personally. But doing so denies something that is part of our very nature.

Our need for small talk starts in the crib between mother and child, well before we can utter a single intelligible syllable. Psychologist and bestselling author Daniel Goleman describes the momentary smiles that occur between mother and child as "protoconversations"—nonverbal exchanges that lay the groundwork for our need to give and get feedback through small, momentary interactions with others. Goleman's research shows how sensitive we are to minute social cues. A baby who looks at his mother and doesn't get the expected smile becomes distressed and withdrawn. These early protoconversations lay the foundation for the ways in which we establish common ground and emotional resonance throughout our lives, with friends, colleagues, family, and strangers.

For Annamarie Ausnes, small talk was, literally, a life-saver.

The Ultimate Coffee Break

Annamarie Ausnes was the kind of person who loved to learn about and remember the little details of everyone's life. One of her favorite haunts was the Starbucks at the corner of North Proctor and 26th Street in Tacoma, Washington. The fifty-five-year-old administrative assistant would stop by each morning on her way to work at a nearby university. Sandie Anderson, the fifty-one-year-old barista who usually served her, didn't know her name but always had her short-drip double-cupped coffee waiting.

Annamarie usually bought her jolt of java with spare change she had accumulated, and in the few moments it usually took her to fish out her quarters, dimes, and nickels, she and Sandie would enjoy a quick, friendly exchange. Through those brief daily conversations, they came to know about grandkids' birthdays, favorite vacation spots, and holiday visits from far-flung relatives.

One morning, however, Sandie could tell that Annamarie wasn't herself. She seemed glum. "What's wrong?" she asked. "Are you feeling okay?" At first, Annamarie was reluctant to tell her, but Sandie gently continued to prod.

Annamarie finally confided, "I was just placed on the national kidney transplant list, and I'm getting ready to go on dialysis." The polycystic kidney disease she had been suffering from for seventeen years had become life threatening, and no donor was available. No one in Annamarie's family was a match, and it would likely be years before she might get a kidney from the organ bank.

"Right away, my first thought was about her new grand-daughter, Ava," Sandie remembers. Sandie had three beloved grandchildren of her own. Looking across the counter at Annamarie, she didn't hesitate.

"I'm going to get tested for you!" she announced.

Annamarie was stunned at the barista's generosity, but tried not to get her hopes up. After all, the odds of Sandie being a match were small. Moreover, the two women barely knew each other. Even if Sandie were a match, Annamarie wouldn't blame her if she backed down. But each day, Sandie assured Annamarie that she was pursuing her offer.

One morning, as Annamarie walked into the store, Sandie couldn't contain her excitement. She reached across the counter and grabbed Annamarie's hand: "I'm a match!" she cried. The two women hugged and began weeping, oblivious to the growing line of bewildered customers.

"We stood there and just bawled," Annamarie remembered later. "The line was stretching practically out the door by then, but it was surreal, like it was just the two of us in the world."

Why would a virtual stranger offer to make such a sacrifice for her? Annamarie comes back to the short conversations they shared every morning. "When you look into someone's eyes, you see a person, and you can connect with their warmth."

Just the few minutes it took each morning to carefully

count out her change had planted the seeds of a deeper friendship. "I never thought a $1.52 cup of coffee would literally save my life," Annamarie says.

Sandie kept her word. The surgery took place on March 11, 2008, and was a success for both recipient and donor. When they woke up, the women couldn't wait to see each other. As Sandie later admitted, with a smile Annamarie has come to treasure, "We just wanted to talk and talk and talk and talk."

We have become so insular as a society that we think there's no need for small talk. We're busy and focused on getting from one place to another, and on achieving results. We forget how important it is to let our armor down and let people see another side of us. Annamarie might have held fast to her initial impulse and kept her problem to herself. What if Sandie hadn't gently persisted? A life literally hung in the balance; the outcome changed because each woman took a small step outside the boundaries of what was expected. Annamarie let herself be vulnerable; Sandie let herself be nosy. One thing we love about their story is how vividly it reminds us to see each other in ways that go beyond the familiar roles we play. We're in such a rush to get things done that we tend to see the people who make cameo appearances in our lives every day solely through the roles they play: They're just the guy who sells us a newspaper every morning, or the woman who takes our dry cleaning. We often don't look beyond the uniform they wear or the service they offer. Making a human connection takes only a few moments, a few words. And a life can sometimes rest in the balance.

Schmooze or Lose

Research suggests that it only takes us about seven seconds to decide how we feel about another person. In business or professional situations, those first few seconds are crucial. "Once someone mentally labels you as 'likeable' or 'unlikeable,' everything else you do will be viewed through that filter. If someone likes you, she'll look for the best in you. If she doesn't like you, she'll suspect devious motives in all your actions," writes Carol Kinsey Goman, author of *The Nonverbal Advantage*.

The ability to excel at small talk can make an enormous difference in how others feel about you. And that can have repercussions down the line both in your career and in your personal life. Dr. Thomas Harrell, a professor at Stanford University, spent much of his career tracking a group of MBAs after graduation. He discovered that their grade-point averages had little effect on their ultimate success in the business world—what really mattered were their conversation skills. The graduates who ended up with the most prestigious jobs and the highest salaries were the ones who were most adept socially.

Our ability to master the art of small talk can be a huge boost to our professional and personal lives, but only if we know how to take advantage of it. Here are a few tips:

Lighten Up

It turns out that kidding around at the beginning of a meeting is one of the most productive things you can do. Seriously.

Chris Robert, a psychologist at the University of Missouri, found that humor in the workplace enhances creativity and job performance. We have noticed this at our agency as well. We begin every creative brainstorming session for a new ad campaign with light banter, or a joke or two. It helps relax the team and brings the stress level in the room down a notch. After all, just try being creative and freewheeling in your thinking when you feel pressured and tense. In fact, as we have recounted many times, goofing around is exactly what made Aflac a household word.

We had been working on campaign ideas for Aflac for weeks. It wasn't easy—the name of the company was difficult to remember. And how interesting could we make insurance? Many of the people working with us on the account were constantly forgetting the name of the company we were pitching (Aflac stands for the American Family Life Assurance Company). Even as we got down to the wire before our big presentation to the CEO, we were feverishly trying to settle on a breakthrough approach. Nothing was jelling. To blow off steam, Eric David, one of our creative directors, decided to take a break and grab lunch at the corner deli. On the walk there, he kept repeating the name—"Aflac-Aflac-Aflac . . ."—over and over to himself. He arrived back at our offices with a corned beef on rye and a smile on his face. He then proceeded to pinch his nose as he quacked out "AFLAC!" at his partner, Tom Amico, and waddled around like a duck.

This might seem like unacceptable behavior at a company not accustomed to the antics of advertising or comedy writing, but we knew we had just seen a brilliant idea hatched before our eyes: making a duck the star of the campaign. We won the account, and the "Aflac duck" has become one of the most famous icons in American advertising.

Just Say Please

An essential ingredient in making small talk is finding a way to make the other person feel special and appreciated. Yet in too many companies, such positive affirmations are ignored altogether.

Sullivan & Cromwell, a staid, white-shoe law firm, had an attrition problem—over 30 percent turnover for two years running. Compensation was not the issue—the lawyers were extremely well paid. Nor were promotions or health benefits at fault. Simply put, the young attorneys did not feel appreciated. When the journal *American Lawyer* published its annual review of midlevel associates, Sullivan & Cromwell ranked near the very bottom of 163 firms surveyed.

So in August of 2006, Sullivan & Cromwell's partners decided to introduce two phrases throughout the company that had been sorely missing from the firm's lexicon: "please" and "thank you." Senior partners began making small talk with junior associates in the halls, over lunch, and in the elevators. They began praising them for jobs well done, or politely asking, rather than demanding, if they would be able to stay late for an urgent meeting.

It didn't cost a dime, but the effort to be gracious, respectful, and polite to everyone in the firm, regardless of their position in the hierarchy, had a powerful effect. When the next *American Lawyer* review rolled around, Sullivan & Cromwell was rated the *top* employer among New York firms. And it all had to do with the power of small talk. The fact is, the words we use to express ourselves—as well as those we don't use—make a big difference on how others perceive us, and feel about us.

Curiosity Kills the Competition

There is nothing more seductive than being around someone who finds you fascinating. It is the secret behind successful talk-show hosts like Jay Leno, who works hard to always make his guests seem brilliant and funny. And that's the reason he gets these guests back, time after time.

Yet when we make small talk, too many of us tend to turn the subject of the conversation quickly back on ourselves, a subject infinitely less interesting to the other person, unless you happen to be Johnny Depp or Angelina Jolie. Leno realizes that asking questions of his guests and making them the center of attention makes them comfortable and more likely to do an effective job entertaining the audience. As he told us, "The trick is to make the guest look good at the expense of the host. The shows that tend to fail are the ones where the host looks good at the expense of the guest. Eventually the host realizes, 'Hey, how come I'm not getting these guests anymore?' "

The results of a recent study conducted by clinical psychology doctoral students Todd Kashdan and Paul Rose revealed that being nosy is a turn-on. The more curious people are during a conversation, the more positive the outcome, whether it is a casual encounter or one where a deeper connection is sought. Either way, the other person feels important and valued, which then has a boomerang effect on the person asking the questions. Who doesn't like being around someone who seems infinitely more interested in our lives than in their own?

We have often been in competition with another top agency for a new account or a piece of business, only to end up winning it because the client felt we were more curious about their company and what makes it tick. Our interest is genuine—we really do want to know and understand the people we would be working with, and the intricacies of their business. The curious thing is that these interactions don't happen in board meetings, they happen during the casual social intercourse or chitchat that precedes a formal presentation. Our point: Small talk is anything but idle chatter. In fact, it's the glue that cements so many relationships.

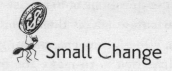

Small Change

EMBRACE "STRANGER DANGER." No one would suggest that you befriend a suspicious six-foot leather-clad man lurking in the subway station. But chatting with the friendly bank teller or with the woman standing behind you in the movie line couldn't hurt. The CEO of a private jet leasing company recently gave up his seat at the counter of his local diner so a dad could sit next to his young daughters. As the CEO began to exchange pleasantries with him, the man remarked that his company was looking to rent a jet on a year-round basis. As a result, the CEO landed a huge account—and all because he decided to make small talk with a total stranger!

PLAY REPORTER. Borrow some tips from successful journalists whose livelihoods depend on getting people to open up. The best reporters learn early on to ask open-ended questions. "So you got out safely?" is likely to get a simple "Yes" in response. "So how did you manage to escape the fire?" not only elicits a far more interesting response, it establishes a connection that will keep the conversation flowing. Another trick of the trade: Resist the natural urge to top someone else's story. People shut down when they sense that the person they're talking to isn't really listening so much as just waiting for their turn to speak. The next time someone shares an anecdote, make yourself ask a question before you launch into your own tale.

GO ON AN E-MAIL DIET. One day a week, try limiting your e-mail output, and ask people in your address book to do the same. Force yourself to engage in more human interaction throughout your workday. We had an "e-mail diet day" at The Kaplan Thaler Group and the results were incredible. The increased banter between employees led to more productive work sessions and made work a lot more fun.

STEER THE CONVERSATION. If you want to find out what happened at the seventh-grade dance last night, don't expect a full report the second your son walks through the door that night. But Dad can probably pick up some details while he's driving Mr. Cool around on the weekend. Kids are famous for telling all—or at least some—while riding in the car. Minivan confessionals, psychologists say, have to do with kids being in their comfort zone, and with being able to talk without having to make eye contact or have their facial expressions read.

Chapter 4

Go the Extra Inch

If you think small things don't matter, think of the last game you lost by one point.
—Anonymous

Robin's husband, Kenny, was a young and ambitious student at New York University, pursuing his degree in health-care administration. Although he still had a semester left before graduation, he was anxious to get his foot in the door someplace and start his career.

The economy was going through a rough patch at the time and jobs, especially entry-level positions, were scarce. But one day, Kenny spotted something that seemed perfect—an evening administrator's post at New York City's prestigious Lenox Hill Hospital. It was a junior job and, because it was a night shift, perfect for a student still in classes during the day. Although the job description specified someone with a little more experience than Kenny had, he decided to apply for it. He spent two weeks preparing for his interview with Lenox Hill administrators, and had become a veritable walking encyclopedia on the history of the hospital. But on the day of his interview, Kenny woke up to a surprise snowstorm. The newscasters were warning that it could be the biggest blizzard in years—as much as two feet of snow was predicted.

Kenny considered canceling, but since hospitals run twenty-four hours a day regardless of the weather, he realized that his interviewer would almost certainly find his way in to work. Dependability was no doubt a major consideration when hospitals were hiring. So he pulled on his L.L. Bean boots and thermal parka and headed out.

Normally the trip from suburban White Plains to East 76th Street in Manhattan, where Lenox Hill was located, took an hour. But Kenny wasn't going to trust his fate to the commuter train schedule. He left three hours ahead of time, to ensure that he would arrive with plenty of time to spare. He caught the train and started going over his notes yet again.

Unfortunately, the snow was falling so hard the train tracks became impassable. Kenny's train stopped midway to Manhattan and stood there. Kenny could only watch helplessly from his frosted window as the world outside was blanketed in white. Soon, he was no longer three hours early; he was nearly an hour late for this crucial interview.

Why didn't Kenny whip out his cell phone and call or text the hospital about his predicament? Well, the year was 1978. There were no cell phones; there wasn't even a pay phone on this train. Kenny grew increasingly agitated at the thought of missing his big opportunity.

Finally, in desperation, he explained his situation to the train conductor and implored him to radio ahead and ask the dispatcher to call the hospital on Kenny's behalf. The conductor took pity on Kenny and put in the call, even though it was against the rules.

Kenny finally showed up at the interview several hours late, disheveled, and wet. The interviewer told Kenny he had received the message, and appreciated Kenny's effort. And then they began to talk.

Kenny thought the interview went well. But, realistically, he didn't have much experience, and there were a lot of candidates for the job. When the hospital finally called days later, he braced himself for bad news. To his surprise, the human resources manager on the other end asked if he was still interested in the position.

"Yes, of course," Kenny replied.

The caller apologized for the delay and explained that the administrators had initially selected someone who seemed more qualified, but at the last moment they had had a change of heart. While it was true that Kenny was the most junior of the people interviewed for the job, his determination to get to the interview—despite a record-breaking snowstorm— had impressed management. In fact, it was what convinced them to offer him the position. After all, the supervisors realized, they could teach Kenny the basic skills needed for the position. But his kind of resourcefulness and commitment to go above and beyond were rare qualities.

Kenny got the job, which proved to be the springboard to a successful career. Today, Kenny is a senior executive at the New York City Health and Hospitals Corporation, the largest municipal hospital system in America.

As employers, we sometimes find ourselves disheartened these days by the sense of entitlement we see in many job seekers entering the market. Young people don't seem to always understand the advantages of going out of their way—going that extra inch—to land a job, or even a piece of business. Dr. Lester Lefton, president of Kent State, finds that even those graduating from business school with straight As often need extra coaching on the minutiae that really count when you're learning how to make an impression in the workplace. "We have to tell them: You need to have polished shoes, wear a tie, no you can't wear flip-flops to meet the president of the United States," he says.

Of course Kenny's interview could have been rescheduled. But he didn't allow himself that sense of entitlement; he had such a sense of commitment, drive, and urgency that nothing could deter him. In some ways, he was given a gift that day—the chance to reveal his character, to prove he would be there no matter what, and that he would not renege on a promise. It was a sneak preview of what kind of employee he would be.

Going the extra inch is that little thing you do that is special and shows what makes you different, what sets you apart from somebody else.

It is often the small act that shows you care, that proves the project or other person matters to you. It affords you a chance to show off your initiative. This can be especially important when you're meeting someone for the first time. Paul Gumbiner, a top-flight corporate recruiter, recites what he calls the "Starbucks Rule." He tells job candidates, "Never show up for an interview with a Starbucks cup, unless you have one for the person you are meeting with."

Strolling in with your own coffee is not only overly casual, it suggests that you presumed your host would lack the manners to offer you anything. "But if you come with an unexpected treat for the other person, like a latte and biscotti," Gumbiner goes on, "you've proved you know how to think about making clients happy before the interview even begins." With that one casual gesture, you send an important message about your natural abilities to anticipate the needs of others and take the initiative.

We know how appreciative our clients are at the extra effort we make to please them. Whether it's the junior art director who canceled her Friday night plans to resize a last-minute layout, or the veteran account supervisor who agreed to temporarily work on-site for one of our Midwest clients who was suddenly short a marketing director. In turn, we enjoy coming up with unique ways to show our appreciation to our own staff—like closing early on Halloween so parents can get home for trick-or-treat. We serve breakfast to our employees on Monday mornings to ease the transition back to the workweek, and we throw a monthly make-your-own-sundae party to celebrate birthdays. These are perks that cost us little but generate enormous gratitude and goodwill from our staff. It tells them we care about their personal time and family time, as well as about getting the work done. These small gestures go a long way toward ensuring an energized esprit de corps if we need to ask our people to work two weekends in a row when we're in a crunch for a new campaign. And it has paid off handsomely for our bottom line: Our employee retention rates are well above the industry average, which is a huge plus when you consider that it costs one-third of a person's annual salary to replace a valued employee.

But it wasn't always smooth sailing for us. As we mentioned earlier, when we started The Kaplan Thaler Group, we had just one account—Clairol Herbal Essences Shampoo. Another agency handled a companion product Clairol was introducing, called Herbal Essences Body Wash. Then we heard through the grapevine that they were having trouble with the campaign. Clairol was worried that the commercial to launch the new body wash product would not be ready for the all-important first airdate on network TV. Although we were up to our ears with our own work and the challenges of a barely two-month-old business, we casually mentioned to Clairol president Steve Sadove, that we would be happy to take a crack at reediting the spot for them—free of charge. So we worked all weekend and completely recut the commercial. And Clairol loved it. Though it wasn't our account, that commercial became the first one The Kaplan Thaler Group put on the air. And a few months later we were officially given the business.

That was eleven years ago. Today, delivering such little extras is no longer just a nice thing to do—it is essential for maintaining a competitive advantage. The Internet, after all, offers infinite choices and instant gratification for clients and customers. No free wireless service at the hotel you planned to check into? Click to the next. Continental Airlines grasped this new reality quickly. The airline business is one of the toughest there is. No one can prevent air traffic delays or guarantee clear skies, but Continental Airlines works hard to compensate by offering passengers a pillow, blanket, and a meal at mealtime when most other airlines have taken these things away. By keeping these amenities, Continental is essentially saying, "We're still grateful for your business."

As a result, Continental's consumer satisfaction ratings are among the top ones in the industry. In 2007, J.D. Power and Associates gave Continental their highest rank for customer satisfaction. And *Fortune* magazine named Continental the number-one airline in their survey of most-admired global airline companies.

"Thank You" Goes a Long Way

When we published our book, *The Power of Nice*, comedian Rosie O'Donnell talked about the principles we describe on network television.

Back in the early eighties, when Rosie was a comedian doing stand-up, she heard about an incredible opportunity: a chance to work with MTV as a VJ. Rosie was a young comic looking for an opportunity to move up from the local clubs to a national audience, so she decided to go for it. She made the first cut and was flown to New York for another audition with one of MTV's top executives.

"I didn't get it," she said. "But I wrote him a thank-you note and said thank you for giving me a shot."

In an industry of outsized egos, such graciousness did not go unnoticed. So the MTV executive took the liberty of forwarding Rosie's audition tape to VH1. Rosie landed that gig, and launched her meteoric rise in television.

Yes, she got the job because of her incredible talent. But VH1 would have never discovered her if it hadn't been for her quick thank-you note and the MTV executive's decision to pass her tape along instead of tossing it aside.

The simple act of saying thank you often determines whether an encounter is experienced as good or bad. Catherine Roster of the University of New Mexico interviewed 186 people who had given a gift the recipient didn't like. There were a number of ways the gift givers came to realize that their waffle makers and polka-dot ties were not a hit. But the one that did the most damage to the relationship was the recipient's failure to say thank you. When asked what the person receiving the gift could have done differently to make the situation better, the gift givers overwhelmingly said a thank you would have done the trick—even if it wasn't genuine!

Getting noticed in a meaningful way is less about the grand gesture and more about the small, thoughtful things we do every day. We've found that there's often a pay-it-forward beauty to going that extra inch. Setting the power of small in motion can be as easy as writing a thank-you note that isn't expected, or asking after your customer's children by name. Too often in our elbows-out world, it's assumed that being considerate and being competitive are mutually exclusive traits. In fact, the opposite is true.

Celebrated restaurateur Danny Meyer makes a point of personally writing at least two notes a day to people dining in his award-winning New York City restaurants. Whether it's to wish someone a happy anniversary, or to congratulate them on a recent promotion, his motivation is simple and heartfelt. "I think in a world where you almost have to multitask just to keep up with the profusion of information coming your way," he tells us, "the human gesture is one of the unfortunate casualties."

He acknowledges his customers in ways they may never realize. For example, when he noticed several lunchtime reservations recently at Union Square Café for people with similar political leanings, Meyer strategically placed them within sight of one another. So former senator Bob Kerrey, once a Democratic presidential hopeful, may have *thought* it was serendipitous to be seated near fund-raisers for Senators Barack Obama and Hillary Clinton, with a former editor of the *Nation* nearby, but it was no coincidence.

"It's chance that they all came to the restaurant on the same day," Meyer explains, "but by paying attention to small details, I can make good things happen for people. We can do this with literary people. We can do this with food people. We can do this with advertising people, political people. And people get up out of their seats, and they may become reacquainted with someone in their own world that they haven't seen for a long time. That then may lead to something else. It all reflects positively back onto having come to Union Square Café or whichever of the restaurants I'm talking about."

Being attentive even when you don't "have to" will sharpen your eye for the kinds of details that can make or break your reputation in the business world. Did you follow up on that niggling detail that has almost certainly already been taken care of, on the off chance it hasn't? Did the messenger service understand that they were to leave that package if there is no doorman? Did the correct e-mail address make it into the ad? Did you acknowledge the contributions of the production staff or marketing folks on that special project? Double-checking is a habit worth developing. "Always check small things" became an absolute rule for General Colin Powell years before he became a respected military commander and, later, secretary of state.

Look Before You Leap

Powell was an army officer training as a Pathfinder, one of the elite paratroopers who jump in ahead of airborne assaults to mark landing and drop zones. On the last day of the course, Powell relates in his autobiography, the officers faced a treacherous night jump from a helicopter after a daylong cross-country march. As they were preparing to jump, Powell, as senior officer on board, yelled at the men over the roar of the engines to check their static lines, which automatically open the parachutes. The lines were supposed to be hooked to a floor cable. Powell called out a second reminder. Then, "like a fussy old woman," he began checking each line himself. A sergeant's was loose. The man would almost certainly have plummeted to his death if Powell hadn't caught the mistake that three men—the paratrooper, his buddy, and the jumpmaster—had already missed. "Never neglect details," Powell writes, "even to the point of being a pest. Moments of stress, confusion, and fatigue are exactly when mistakes happen."

Pay a Little More Attention

We often *think* about taking that extra step. A nagging thought crosses our minds as we're racing to complete nine other tasks, worrying over how far behind we are on the day's to-do list. Unfortunately, we don't heed that inner voice. We forget. Or we get too busy, and that mental Post-it gets lost in the tsunami of other demands. We neglect to completely finish one job to our full satisfaction before diving into the next. Everyone you know is suffering from the same time crunched challenges. We've all found ourselves on the phone with someone only to hear the telltale sound of a keyboard clicking away in the background. And we've all done it ourselves at one time or another. Whether it's legitimate multitasking or an unscheduled cyber recess, the pace of today's workweek seems to demand it at times.

Author Daniel Goleman refers to this phenomenon as the "I–It" interaction, a term first coined by philosopher Martin Buber. By not fully paying attention to the other person and his or her needs, we deny ourselves the opportunity to create empathy and an emotional attachment with the other person. According to Dr. Goleman, "When other tasks or preoccupations split our attention, the dwindling reserve left for the other person we are talking with leaves us operating on automatic, paying just enough attention to keep the conversation on track."

No wonder the "I–It" interaction takes place with increasing frequency, at work and at home. It's harder to pay attention in an ADD (attention deficit disorder) world. We're surrounded by computer screens, BlackBerrys, cell phones, TVs, iPods, and bustling people and their demands— all of them crying, "Look at me!" At work, they thwart even our best intentions to focus on and complete the job at hand—much less overdeliver. We may be the first generation to find that more information is actually making us dumber, and less productive. Harvard psychiatrist Edward Hallowell has invented a new name for this information-age syndrome—Attention Deficit Trait" or ADT. Unlike attention deficit disorder, which has biological causes, ADT is a syndrome we give to ourselves. Hallowell claims that ADT makes us increasingly distracted, irritable, and restless—and, over the long term, underachieving. It amounts to a form of self-inflicted failure. If we want to give a little extra to our job, to a project, to other people, to our family, we need to stop trying to do so many things at once.

To help avoid Attention Deficit Trait disasters at The Kaplan Thaler Group, we abide by the "Read twice, send once" rule. It may seem obvious, or even trivial, but it speaks to an entire mind-set we foster at KTG: Pause. Take that extra minute to make sure the address is correct, or that the invoice you sent to a supplier was actually received. Did you know that a small percentage of digital correspondence actually "gets lost" in cyberspace? As anyone who has ever tried frantically to retrieve an errant e-mail can tell you, taking that extra twenty seconds to be a persnickety proofreader is one of the most valuable things you can do. It helped Robin avoid a near disaster recently.

As many BlackBerry Pearl owners know, instead of a full keyboard, it has two letters assigned to each key. The software uses a program called Smart Type to figure out which letter you want. For example, the "I" and the "U" are on the same key. Well, a year ago I wrote a long e-mail to our Aflac client summarizing some of the many commercials we had produced using the Aflac D-U̲-C-K. Unfortunately my BlackBerry had something a little naughtier in mind. If I hadn't taken those few extra seconds to proofread my message, we would have had a very X-rated e-mail to explain to one of our most important clients.

Take Advantage of the Smallest Opportunities

The opportunity to go beyond what is expected can crop up unexpectedly and in unexpected ways, as Michelle Alba-Lim found out. She is the founder of a small business, WLF Interactive Development Centre. Her fledgling training and consulting firm has a phone number very similar to that of a nearby movie theater. As a result, Michelle frequently received calls from people trying to reach the theater for show times and information.

She was working late one day when the phone rang in her office.

"The woman on the other end wanted to know the time for the last screening of *Beauty and the Beast*," Michelle says. "I was taking my kids to that same show, so instead of telling her that she'd dialed the wrong number, I gave her the information she needed and added that traffic was very heavy in the area so she should allow an extra half hour to get to the theater and find parking."

Michelle then gave the woman the theater's correct phone number, and asked her to make a note of it. She heard a long pause on the other end of the line.

"If this isn't Greenhill's Theatre, why did you give me all that information? Who is this?"

Michelle explained to the perplexed caller that she ran the WLF Interactive Development Centre, and that their phone number was very similar to the theater's. They exchanged some pleasantries and said good-bye.

She thought that was the last time she would ever hear from the caller.

But to her surprise, a few days later, a young woman called on behalf of her boss and hired Michelle to train their staff in how to use telephones effectively. Says Michelle, "The small effort I had taken to give a little extra information had created such a favorable impression that her boss engaged me to conduct a training seminar without even meeting me in person!"

Such random acts of kindness can sometimes pay off in surprising ways. Program yourself to keep your "small" antennae up throughout the day to catch those serendipitous opportunities. Psychologist Mosha Belkin believes that our emotional and social instincts can be trained and developed in the same way as our biceps and triceps. You may feel a little awkward at first as you begin to pay more attention to the people around you and to their behavior and conversations. But with practice, you will get better at automatically noticing opportunities to go above and beyond and do more than expected. Believe us, people will remember you if you do—and you'll feel better and more engaged with those around you as well.

Pushing yourself just a little harder is one of the great hidden keys to company and career success, as well as to building better friendships and stronger relationships. Sam Walton, the founder of Wal-Mart, was famous for flying around the country in his helicopter to personally visit hundreds of Wal-Mart stores every year. His chopper would land in the parking lot and Sam would stride into the store and ask employees: "How may I help you?" He knew that the motivation and commitment of his employees directly impacted the success of his company. Whether you're in retail, real estate, research, or any business in which you interact with clients and customers, going the extra inch can be an enormously powerful catalyst for positive change.

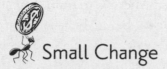 Small Change

DO THE WRITE STUFF. When was the last time you got a letter in the mail? In the not-too-distant past, handwritten notes from friends were a high point of everyday life. E-mail has become so routine, though, that convenience has trumped convention. Nowadays, finding anything more personal than a Pottery Barn catalog in the mail is rare. But that spells an opportunity for you: You can be that rare gem among the daily slag of bills and credit-card offers. People are all the more surprised and delighted when a handwritten note does appear in the mailbox. If you want to make a positive impression, take the few extra minutes to pick up a pen and write a note. You're more likely to become memorable instead of merely deleted.

SIGN UP. Offer to do something "extra" regularly. It can be as modest as giving your spouse a break by volunteering to take the dog for a walk on a rainy night, or helping your co-worker get a rush project down to FedEx. Such gestures may take only a few minutes, but their effects can last a career or a lifetime.

ADD A MINUTE. When you've completed a task, a memo, a quarterly budget—anything that you're just glad to be done with—stop and tell yourself you still have one minute left. Spend just those sixty seconds rereading a troublesome paragraph, or adding up the numbers again. You may be glad you did.

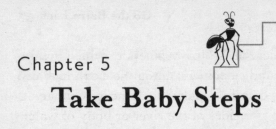

Chapter 5
Take Baby Steps

The greatest things ever done on Earth have been done little by little.
—William Jennings Bryan

One hundred and sixty years ago, Niagara Falls was not only a spectacular natural wonder, it was an impassable obstacle. The United States and Canada were eager to capitalize on the magnificent falls they shared, but both tourism and commerce were hindered by the lack of a bridge between the two sides. The gorge between the two cliffs was too wide and whirlpool waters of the Niagara River too deep for ships to safely navigate anywhere near the falls, and the only passageway was a small ferry that crossed way upstream. If only they could build a bridge spanning the breathtaking divide, and make the falls a major tourist attraction, the benefit to both countries would be tremendous. But the idea was swiftly dismissed by the leading engineers of Europe and North America as unviable. Only a few believed it could be done. One engineer who did was a brash young man from Philadelphia named Charles Ellet Jr., who had a passion for suspension bridges.

Suspension bridges are a tricky deal. They must be

strong enough to hold tons of weight—but, ironically, the construction of such a massive-scale project is generally begun with a single cable. Typically, engineers will string a wire between the two sides of the river or body of water, and then build on that small step repeatedly until the cables are powerful enough to safely hold a great deal of weight. But when it came to spanning Niagara Falls, with 800 feet to cross and jagged cliffs towering 225 feet high, Ellet's team was stymied. Fastening a thick cable to one side of the gorge and carrying it across by boat to the other side was impossible because of the treacherous rapids. Over dinner one night, Ellet's team bandied about complex and intricate suggestions as to how to surmount that obstacle. Ellet speculated on whether a rocket might work. Someone else proposed sending the wire across via cannonball. But these ideas were soon dismissed as impractical. After all, the goal was to bridge Canada, not bomb it.

Problem-solving Is Child's Play

Ultimately, the winning solution came not from a member of the team of experienced engineers, but a local man. His idea was so logical that it was ridiculously simple—or simply ridiculous. How about a kite-flying contest? If one of the kites made it over the river, its line could be anchored on the other side, and used to pull across increasingly heavier and stronger lines. Finally, a steel cable could be pulled across by steam winch and secured in place to serve as a foundation for a suspension bridge. The first person to fly a kite across the river would reap a $10 prize—big money at the time. The contest would run until someone succeeded.

Over the following months, dozens of kite flyers tried their luck. The competitors persisted even through an icy winter. Finally, an American boy named Homan Walsh got a kite he had named "The Union" across the river. "We have this day joined the United States and Canada with a cord, half an inch in diameter," the *Buffalo Daily Courier* recorded on January 31, 1848. Six months later, on August 1, 1848, the Niagara Falls Suspension Bridge was open to the public.

It was a feat that had seemed insurmountable. The solution was to solve it as a series of small problems. That's how the local guy was able to figure out what a team of trained experts could not: Because while they were trying to figure out the big job—how to erect a bridge—he focused his energy on solving the smallest part of that daunting task: getting a string across a river.

A Nobel Prize winner once calculated that each day consists of 20,000 waking moments. The key is to fully occupy each one, and focus on what needs your attention now, rather than obsessing about the mammoth projects or problems looming ahead. You can always cross that bridge when you come to it.

Chipping Away

While problem-solving is often viewed as an intricate, convoluted process—and there are as many theories on problem-solving as there are problems—often, the right solution is the simplest one. In 1945, a man named George Pólya published a book with Princeton University that was called *How to Solve It*. Pólya's modest little volume discussed how to solve problems—specifically, math problems. But his ideas are just as useful for those of us who don't spend our spare time doing calculus. "If you can't solve a problem," says Pólya, "then there is an easier problem you can solve: Find it." In other words, look first for some "related problem" before attacking the tougher one. Pólya's simple advice has held steadfast for generations now—his book, translated into several languages, has sold over a million copies and never gone out of print.

When a major task or massive project looms, it's natural to feel overwhelmed at first, or to imagine that only a comprehensive solution can provide the needed fix. And when we start looking for answers to those questions, insecurity and fear of failure can be paralyzing, stopping us in our tracks. That's when crippling procrastination sets in, and it seems impossible to even get started. You're caught in a chain-reaction of your own inaction.

The answer, we've found, is to re-imagine the project from the outset: Mentally dismantle the challenge into smaller, less formidable pieces.

That's also how we approach our advertising challenges at KTG. By downsizing the mountains into manageable molehills, we can surmount any problem. For example, it's a daunting task to invent a new annual ad campaign for a client. That's why we'll often start the big assignment by zeroing in on an idea for a single print ad or digital banner. One clever headline begins to inspire another, and soon we're all trying to one-up each other with our individual contributions to the campaign. We all feed off the collective energy. That's exactly how we approached the creation of our 2007 "No Worries" campaign for Outback Restaurants. Although the largest part of our assignment was a batch of expensive new TV commercials, we started off with a couple of silly ideas for bar coasters—arguably one of the least-critical elements of the task. The first one the creative team came up with said on the front "I Googled myself and found nothing," and "No Worries" on the back. Another said, "Let us know if you valet parked. We don't have valet parking." Within days we had gone from bar coasters to ideas for newspaper ads, billboards, TV spots, and a new website, all based on the "No Worries" theme. And doing it one small element at a time took a lot of "worries" out of our lives.

Order in the House

The same approach works at home as well as at the office. Molly Boren, owner of Simplicity Works Organizing Services in Chicago, remembers the desperate call she got from a busy homeowner named Rebecca, who felt overwhelmed by the clutter in her family's large three-story house. "It was a fairly typical case," Molly remembers. "She had a busy family, she was working from her home, and she had a lot of craft projects going on—scrapbooking, knitting, jewelry-making." Rebecca had tried to get things in order many times, but whatever success she achieved was inevitably short-lived, and the piles and heaps and stacks of "stuff" took over again.

When Molly visited, she wasn't surprised to discover

that the basement was the real nightmare zone. "The floor was pretty-much covered with junk—musical instruments, beading supplies, a lot of paper, memorabilia for scrapbooks. The floor and all table surfaces were covered with projects in process. But the projects had been stalled because there was no more surface to work on."

As a pro, Molly knew exactly how to tackle the mess, and reorganize, but she also knew better than to dive into the deep end. Instead, she led her new client back upstairs, and zeroed in on the desk in the kitchen. That, too, was covered with papers. The cabinets were stuffed with a jumble of office supplies, household gadgets, and stray knickknacks. Reorganizing the entire house would take months, Molly knew, but this desk would only take a few hours. "The best way to start is to isolate one small project and allow enough time to work on it from start to finish," Molly advises. Being able to complete that first task relatively quickly gave Rebecca a feeling of both satisfaction and motivation. They moved on to the pantry, then increasingly larger spaces in the house, with Molly sectioning each off into a doable chunk. "Even when you're ready to start the biggest task—in this case, the basement—you should start with the smallest part," Molly says. "A lot of people tend to overload themselves and work harder than they are comfortable doing. And then you get tired and it's kind of painful, and so the idea I share with my clients is to move the ball down the field as opposed to running it for a touchdown. Zoom in on one corner, or the basement stairs. If there are five things to do in that corner, you have something tangible, but it also has limits."

Pulling back every once in a while to see how far you've gotten is also important, "because you can see your accomplishments within the big picture, instead of measuring yourself against the larger, scarier reality."

Thinking Japanese

Numerous studies show that all kinds of "change" programs, whether they focus on health, career, relationships, or personal growth, are most successful when participants focus on frequent, *achievable* little goals. Twelve-step programs have a well-documented record of success helping people take control of negative behaviors, including alcohol abuse (Alcoholics Anonymous), "shop-till-you-drop" syndrome (Overspenders Anonymous), and even staying too late at the office (Workaholics Anonymous). They build confidence through a continuous series of small successes, exhorting members to approach their problems "one day at a time."

In a similar way, the success of the Japanese auto industry can be traced to the eastern philosophy of "kaizen" and Taoist wisdom, which both hold a view of success as a continuum rather than a singular, distant goal. That belief is best captured in the ancient phrase that has become a modern mantra in personal and career coaching: "The journey of a thousand miles begins with one small step." Instead of using top-down, command-and-control techniques where huge goals are set by management, and employees are expected to submissively carry them out, the kaizen approach empowers workers to focus on opportunities for incremental change, and to constantly look for small improvements. The kaizen method is the foundation for such well-known management programs as Total Quality Control and Six Sigma, and is the force behind Toyota's climb to become the number one automaker in the world.

Dr. Robert Maurer, an associate clinical professor at the UCLA School of Medicine, specializes in the psychology of success, and is a fierce advocate of the power of kaizen in personal as well as professional spheres. As Maurer and other experts explain, kaizen is believed to circumvent the brain's built-in resistance to new behavior through small, conscientious steps.

"The fear of change is rooted in the brain's physiology, and when fear takes hold, it can prevent creativity, change, and success," Maurer explains in his book, *One Small Step Can Change Your Life: The Kaizen Way*. The problem, according to Maurer, is that the structure of the brain that governs this fight-or-flight response—the amygdala—sounds the alarm *whenever* we "want to make a departure from our usual, safe routines . . . Whether the challenge is a new job or just meeting a new person, the amygdala alerts parts of the body to prepare for action—and our access to the cortex, the thinking part of the brain, is restricted, and sometimes shut down." That's why you draw a sudden blank when the CEO flags you down in the hallway to ask about your groundbreaking new proposal, for example. Or why writer's block can stymie even the most talented novelists. We need access to the cortex to flip our creative switches.

The kaizen theory suggests that taking small steps engages the cortex, and prompts the brain to start laying down new nerve pathways to your desired change, building a neurological detour around the flight-or-fight roadblock. In effect, these tiny, almost imperceptible changes we make fool the amygdala into believing that no real change is occurring.

Take Small Rewards

Smaller, more attainable goals will also give you quicker, more frequent mini-rewards. Those early successes, and the sense of gratification they bring, will spur you on to the next task, and the next. Sports psychologists use the same technique to help Olympic athletes reach their peak performance.

If you're running a marathon, track coaches will tell you the last thing you want to do is dwell on how far the race is—26.2 miles—or you'll taste defeat before the gun even goes off. The way to win is to break the race down into a series of manageable distances.

"You are always capable of doing more," says Dr. Bill Morgan, a professor of kinesiology at the University of Wisconsin. Professional athletes with challenging goals have learned to utilize the power of small in their training and in competition.

That's how Paula Radcliffe, three-time winner of the New York and London marathons, as well as the winner of the marathon at the 2005 World Championship, reaches the finish line—and the winners' circle. She never lets herself think, "one more mile to go," or "another forty minutes." Instead she counts every footfall. "When I count to a hundred three times, it's a mile," she says. "It helps me focus on the moment and not think about how many miles I have to go." By enjoying each small, achievable goal—just one step at a time—she can distract her mind and keep her body moving.

Linda uses the same theory with her despised Stairmaster:

Setting the timer for my daily 45-minute session fills me with more dread than drive, to be honest. So I set it for just 10 minutes instead. When the ten minutes is up, I reset the timer for nine minutes, then eight, then seven minutes, on down the clock. The amount of time I spend exercising is the same, but I'm a lot more motivated when I get to pat myself on the back and reward myself by making each interval a minute shorter.

Victory is just sweeter—and thighs slimmer—when you savor it bite by bite.

Our point? Small steps can make a huge difference. Every January, Americans make lists of their resolutions for the upcoming year: Get a better job, lose weight, save money, lower cholesterol, find the perfect partner. Of course, most of these grand plans have fallen by the wayside long before Groundhog Day cards start appearing in the aisles. That's because these resolutions are too big, and focus on results rather than taking action. "Lose ten pounds" is a goal, but it doesn't help us accomplish that goal. Genuine, lasting change occurs when people focus on frequent, *achievable* little goals.

So if you're trying to drop a few pounds, make a promise you know you can keep. You don't have to go to a spa, have your stomach stapled, buy expensive sneakers or exist on a diet of cabbage and bouillon. All you need to do is consume 100 calories less a day than you usually do. Over the course of a year, that equals ten pounds. Just replace a glass of juice with water, or a glass of wine with seltzer, or a piece of cake with an apple. Or burn it off: Take a two-mile walk or vacuum the living room and do a load of laundry. Even such slight adjustments to what you eat and how you exercise can shrink your waistline over the course of a few months.

And don't forget that small change can pay off in a big way literally as well as figuratively. Who wouldn't like to find some extra money these days? While you're daydreaming about winning the lottery, you might want to first check between the sofa cushions. Coinstar, Inc. estimates there is more than $10.5 billion in loose change sitting idle in American homes. That no longer includes the 1,308,459 pennies that an Alabama gas station attendant spent 38 years collecting. Besides setting a world record for penny-saving, Edmond Knowles can now count on an extra $13,000 to supplement his Social Security. In Indiana, Paul Brant has bought two new pickup trucks and a car so far with the quarters he collects in empty water jugs, coffee cans, piggy banks, and other containers. His stash of cash? A total of nearly $63,000 since 1994. Robin still has a way to go to match that, but her habit of scooping the spare change from the bottom of her purse and dropping it into a jar on her dresser adds up to $15 or more when she makes her monthly stop at her nearby coin-counting machine. Some banks now offer credit cards that automatically round each of your purchases up to the nearest dollar, putting the extra change into your savings account. It adds up quickly, and provides a pleasant surprise each month when you discover that you really spent, say, $50 less than you thought you did—and have been earning interest on it, to boot.

This "small steps" philosophy can have a major impact not only on our financial and physical fitness, but on the way our children learn. There isn't a parent who doesn't spend time thinking—and worrying—about their kids and the way they are doing in school. Families spend thousands of dollars to hire private tutors, or enroll their children in after-school programs that teach them how to take tests. Educators and parents spend long hours going over lessons and homework in an attempt to motivate young minds. But recent research suggests that one easy way to better inspire your children is to make a small change in the way that you praise them. Instead of telling your offspring that they are smart or talented, compliment them on trying hard. This small shift in attitude can have a big impact on how kids approach challenges later on. That's what psychologist Carol Dweck discovered in her seminal, 10-year study of New York public school children. Dweck and her team from Columbia University found that students who were praised for effort instead of natural abilities said things like "I love a challenge" when faced with a problem. This was in opposition to the students who were told how smart they were, who were more likely to walk away from a difficult puzzle. When you take small actions, you pretty much assure yourself of succeeding, which makes you want to take more of those actions.

Author Amy Sutherland discovered this while researching a book about exotic animal trainers, then went on to test her newfound knowledge on her unwitting husband. After years of marriage, she already knew that nagging only seemed to make any annoying habits or behavior worse. "He'd drive faster instead of slower; shave less frequently, not more; and leave his reeking bike garb on the bedroom floor longer than ever," she wrote in a *New York Times* essay that spawned her next book, *What Shamu Taught Me About Life, Love, and Marriage.*

Watching animal trainers achieve the seemingly impossible—like teaching baboons to skateboard—made Sutherland realize that "I should reward behavior I like and ignore behavior I don't." Back home, she began thanking her spouse if he threw a single dirty shirt into the hamper. If he tossed in two, she kissed him. Sutherland held her tongue about the dirty clothes still on the floor.

"I was using what trainers call 'approximations,' rewarding the small steps toward learning a whole new behavior," she reported. "You can't expect a baboon to learn to flip on command in one session, just as you can't expect an American husband to begin regularly picking up his dirty socks by praising him once for picking up a single sock." But it's a good place to start.

Whether your goal is to perk up your relationship, conquer the clutter in your closet or re-energize your business, we can all benefit by cutting what we do into bite-size pieces.

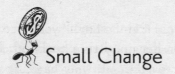

Small Change

RECLAIM LOST MINUTES. We often fantasize about having more hours in the day, or more days in the week. But if you think smaller, you can actually reclaim some lost time. In her state of perpetual jet lag from all the traveling she does, Robin knows she needs to get to bed two hours earlier than she does. But resetting a body clock is tricky. So she resets her body's clock by going to sleep five minutes earlier each day. Within a few weeks, she's back on schedule. If your problem is getting up in the morning, try this in reverse. Before long, you will have found that hour you've been looking for to exercise, or finally get that nagging project off your desk.

PENNIES FOR YOUR THOUGHTS. If you have kids, give each a jar and tell them any change they find is theirs to cash in once the container is full—you'll never find spare dimes in the dryer or on the car floor again. Or turn it into your own personal contest: See how much loose change you can collect in three months, then see if you can double it in six. Keep going and eventually that dream trip to Italy may be within reach. All it takes is a little common cents.

STEALTH CLEANING. Professional organizer Molly Boren tells clients to control clutter by making it a habit to put away three things in the morning and three things at night. Keep a "donations" bag in your closet, toy closet, or garage. When you come across those pants that make your thighs look like kielbasas, toss it in the bag. If you're confronting a major debris field in your playroom, home office, or basement, try making a spyglass with your hand. Look through the "viewfinder" and zero in on that one small area to clean.

Chapter 6

Watch Your Cue(s) and Clues

The more faithfully you listen to the voice within you, the better
you hear what is sounding outside.
—Dag Hammarskjöld

In 1992, when a cargo ship hit a heavy storm near the International Date Line and a dozen containers plunged into the Pacific, it seemed unlikely that anyone but maritime insurance adjusters would take note. After all, what did it really matter in the grand scheme of things if twenty-nine thousand plastic bathtub toys bound for the United States from a toy manufacturer in Hong Kong were adrift at sea?

Since then, smiling yellow duckies have been washing up on shores around the globe, pushed merrily along by wind, waves, and currents. The plucky duckies are known to have ridden ice packs across the North Pole, and to have surfed the waters of Hawaii. They swam with wild salmon off Scotland, and with humpback whales off Maine. They bobbed up on the Alaskan shore by the hundreds and promptly found new homes in hot tubs across Sitka.

Most people walking along a beach would never give a second thought to a faded plastic bath toy sitting in the

sand. Chances are good that you would ignore it altogether, considering it nothing more than flotsam along a
littered shore. But the little toys have a surprising story to
tell from their adventures on the high seas. And they speak
volumes about the oft-hidden power of small. In fact, they
have proven to be a scientific windfall.

When Seattle oceanographers Curtis Ebbesmeyer and
James Ingraham heard about the cargo loss, they recognized
it as more than just a mere accident: It was a huge opportunity. Relying on a worldwide network—and hundred-dollar
bounties—to retrieve the three-inch castaways, the two researchers have entered data into a National Oceanic and
Atmospheric Administration computer model to track the
toys' odyssey so far. Why bother? Because the resilient plastic playthings yield important clues to the mysteries of surface currents.

"The surface of the ocean is more of an unknown than
the bottom," Ebbesmeyer told the *Washington Post*. "It's an
oceanographic blind spot." But the drifting duckies are
helping to change that. By collecting data on where and
when the toys beach, the scientists can better understand
where the oceans' currents are flowing, how fast, and how
and when they interconnect. That kind of information,
in turn, helps predict severe weather, like hurricanes, ty-
phoons, and even droughts.

Ebbesmeyer and Ingraham rely on the power of small to
provide critical clues to one of oceanography's great mysteries. Explains Dr. Ebbesmeyer: "Every item that makes
it to shore has a story to tell and data to impart."

The beachcomber approach is a useful model in other
aspects of our lives as well. We're surrounded by inter-

esting and important cues and clues that might help us to solve our everyday problems and looming challenges. But those indicators typically go unnoticed. We're too busy to stop and look around, and far more inclined to dismiss this kind of minutiae than to explore it. But understanding the bigger picture—whether it's how to track a hurricane or pick the right school for your child—means examining the hundreds or thousands of smaller pieces first. It takes a keen eye to take in such subtle messages in a hectic world. We have to consciously train ourselves to be constantly on the lookout for them, and to react with lightning speed. At times, picking up on a small cue has saved an important piece of business for us at KTG, and clinched an important new deal. We've been known to switch gears in the middle of major presentations because one of us noticed a client sneaking glances at his watch, or nodding appreciatively over some point we had considered incidental.

"One time we were giving a presentation to some prospective clients," recalls Linda, "and I noticed a surprising response when I made a fleeting reference to 'scientific findings.' This guy lit up, and I saw him nudge the person next to him and whisper something in his ear." Using that as a cue, Linda immediately regrouped to take advantage of the information she had just gleaned: She turned her planned remarks inside out to emphasize the scientific aspects of our information. We won not only the account, but a valuable insight into the client's team as well. On his way out the door, the satisfied executive who had nudged his colleague made it clear that we had just validated his own ideas about what direction their advertising should take. Being able to react swiftly to subtle nuances isn't a matter of perfecting your improv skills: It's about becoming adept at recognizing and responding to the often overlooked subtle stimuli that can alert you to what's around the next corner, and give you and your team that extra edge. That skill can come in handy when navigating relationships, as well.

For several months our friend Sandra had been dating a man who appeared to be thoughtful, charming, and generous. But while driving in his car one summer night, they had a near accident that was clearly his fault. Sandra naturally expected that his first response would be to make sure that she was okay, and then perhaps to apologize for his carelessness. Instead, he became furious with the other driver and proceeded to curse him out, never once accepting responsibility or demonstrating any real compassion. There is a Hebrew proverb that says a man's true character is revealed when he is angry. That incident clued her in to his real nature and she ended the relationship—as soon as she was safely home.

Put Your Instincts in Drive

The late Juan Fangio is a legend in the world of auto racing. Known as "El Maestro," the Argentine driver won five Formula One World Driver's Championships—a record that remained unbeaten for forty-six years. It wasn't just his physical reflexes and considerable skill behind the wheel that made him a champion, though. Acuity played a key role.

Back in 1950, Fangio was struggling to make a comeback after spending years off the racetrack. He returned to the racing world with fire in his eyes, determined to become a star yet again. Critics suggested that, at thirty-eight, he was well past his prime, and unlikely to pose much of a threat to younger competitors. Undaunted, Fangio headed to the French Riviera to race in the famous Monaco Grand Prix.

The race is staged in the ancient streets that wind above the Mediterranean, creating one of the more formidable courses in the world. Spectators along the route love their proximity to the race cars, shouting cheers over the din of the roaring engines.

When the race opened, Fangio shot out in front, taking the lead. On his second lap around the course, Fangio suddenly had a funny feeling. He couldn't see around the curve ahead but something just didn't seem right. Instinctively, he hit the brakes.

Just beyond the blind curve, unknown to Fangio, a wave splashing over the road had caused nine cars, still on their first lap, to skid out of control. Fangio's screeching halt—based on that funny feeling he had—prevented him from crashing into the massive pileup. Asked about it later, he remembered a few fleeting things that had contributed to his flash of intuition: First, he recalled looking up at the crowd as he accelerated into the turn. He noticed that they weren't cheering; everyone was looking at something beyond Fangio's view. Second, he remembered having seen an old photograph earlier that day, showing the track in 1936 and an accident in that very same location. Although he wasn't consciously aware of putting two and two together, Fangio's brain processed the data, giving the driver an uneasy feeling that caused him to slam on the brakes.

Fangio went on to win the Monaco Grand Prix that year.

In the modern world, we often have to move at warp speed—if not with the reflexes of a Grand Prix driver—and that's tough to do if we don't rely on our instincts. Those instincts have been honed by years of experiences and recognition of previous circumstances. Too often we've got our foot on the accelerator practically 24/7. So how do we know when to hit the brakes? To react to something that may not yet be obvious?

The answer is simple: Slow down. Tune in to the signals around you. External clues are important, but so are our internal cues.

Cognitive researchers and neuroscientists have spent decades studying perception, intuition, and the ways that we process information. Originally, our brains were thought to capture information like a video camera, and store it for later retrieval. But that simplistic theory has given way to a more complex understanding of our neural circuitry. British psychologist Guy Claxton explored intuition in his book *Hare Brain, Tortoise Mind: Why Intelligence Increases When You Think Less*. He showed that most of our everyday intelligence "belongs not to the screen of consciousness, but to the invisible 'motherboard' behind it."

What Claxton calls "unconscious intelligence" comes about when we hit our mental pause buttons. That's when our brains recognize patterns, or connect the dots, to make sense out of complex situations. It gives meaning to things that may not yet be able to be clearly articulated. When that information does find its way to our conscious minds, it's often in the form of one of those "a-ha!" moments.

That's what happened to world-renowned restaurateur Danny Meyer when he was taking his first fly-fishing lesson. "I wasn't so much fascinated by the actual action of catching a fish," he remembers. "But what I was fascinated with was how it's done. The way you learn which fly to tie is that you wade out into the water and you pick up a stone and you turn it over and you see—you have to look very, very closely—what larvae are actually hatching underneath that rock. Once you see that, that tells you exactly what is actually happening in nature at that moment. That's what kind of fly you have to tie, if you wanna catch fish, 'cause you can't fool the fish." He carried this discovery back into the work world: "You can't fool people. If you're not willing to care about that small of a detail, someone else is gonna catch more fish than you are."

Danny's epiphany didn't come in a hot New York City restaurant kitchen—his natural habitat—but in the middle of a trout stream while on vacation. He went back to work and applied what he learned there—from larvae beneath a rock—to his business. Meyer no longer merely greeted his guests and thanked them for coming to his restaurants; he learned everything he could about them, via the Internet and the media, and from talking to them at their tables, and made decisions accordingly. When we're wooing a new client, we know Danny would never seat a business rival within eavesdropping range. How can we be so sure? Because we know he looks under the rocks.

We Have Five Senses for a Reason

Scientists estimate that one billion stimuli are sent to our brains every second, each of them tied to one of our five senses. If you're walking down a city block, you might, in a single second, hear a bus wheezing, sirens blaring, people shouting. You might smell a passing whiff of coffee or a businessman's musky aftershave. But of the billion stimuli collected in that single second, your brain will select only about one hundred sensations for further processing. When you trust in that personal filtering system and follow the cues it offers, you'll discover that you often "know" more than you know.

Long before focus groups and market research became commonplace, Linda relied on her goose bumps to cue her in on a brilliant ad or idea. "Chills are how I ran the Kodak business for many, many years," she says, laughing. When a Kodak ad or commercial gave her chills or brought a tear to her eye, she knew she'd nailed it. It's not that Linda is clairvoyant. It's because she knows that when an emotional reaction is strong enough to elicit a physical response, it's proof positive you've tapped into something universal and deeply felt. Even now, scores of successful campaigns later, it's common knowledge around our offices that one way to know we've hit on something powerful is if Linda gets goose bumps. "That just gave me chills" continues to tell us more than any in-depth market research ever will. Visceral reactions are often subtle, and fleeting, but they are powerful.

At the FBI Academy in Quantico, Virginia, forensic psychologist Anthony Pinizzotto spent many years teaching what is known as intuitive policing. From his early days as a rookie cop in Washington, D.C., he had been fascinated by the role intuition played in law enforcement. One patrol partner in particular was famous in the department for spotting stolen cars and giving chase even before dispatch radioed back to confirm his hunch. "How do you do that?" Pinizzotto remembers asking him. It turned out that his partner was subconsciously registering little details that were "off," like a driver averting his eyes when the police car passed, or one of the two screws missing from the license plate (a clue that it had been switched).

"There are signals being sent constantly between officers and offenders," Pinizzotto tells us. He calls these signals "microbehaviors."

The importance of teaching law enforcement officers how to recognize and react to these microbehaviors can literally be a matter of life and death. One case Pinizzotto and fellow researchers Edward Davis and Charles Miller III reviewed in their study of violent assaults against officers involved an undercover drug sting. On a warm summer evening in D.C. narcotics officers converged on an open-air drug market. The crowd of dealers and buyers scattered. One of the officers suddenly pointed to a man about thirty feet away and began shouting: "Get the one in the red shirt! He's got a gun!" No weapon was visible, but when police chased the suspect down, they indeed found a handgun hidden in his waistband.

At first, the officer who spotted the suspect couldn't explain how he had known about the gun. "I just knew," he told his superiors. But hunches don't stand up in court.

When he was debriefed about the incident in more detail, the officer described the subtle cues that had alerted him to the danger. The suspect had been sitting on a curb when police arrived, and the officer had noticed him adjust his waistband as he stood up. It was a gesture instinctively familiar to anyone who has carried a gun. Second, even though the night was warm, the suspect was wearing a long-sleeved shirt with the shirttails hanging out. Finally, the officer remembered how the suspect had immediately turned his body to the right, away from the policemen's view, as he began hurrying away. The combination of those "microbehaviors" led the officer to correctly conclude that the man was armed.

Learning to scope out a situation, to take note of and take action on minute details instead of looking for the obvious is a skill often undervalued in today's culture. How often have you heard someone say, "Let's not get bogged down in these details now"? If you don't get bogged down in the details now, they very well may bob up as big problems later. You have to force yourself to focus on and immerse yourself in the minutiae, rather than always looking at the big picture. Those tiny details or easily overlooked cues are trying to tell you something. And the message can't always be put into words.

Pay Attention to the Signals

We communicate in so many ways beyond the spoken word. Similarly, there are many ways to miscommunicate. There is a cautionary tale we like to share with new members of our team at KTG, because it so perfectly captures the importance of accurately interpreting the cues you pick up. Our friend Jody, to her everlasting chagrin, failed to do that during a big presentation to a client. Jody was talking away when she caught the eye of one of the executives listening to the pitch. He winked at her. Feeling cocky about this silent validation of her ideas, Jody quickly winked back in agreement. When she looked over a few minutes later, the exec winked again, and she winked back. "He loves the work. I'm on a roll," she thought. Just before they took a break, the exchange happened for a third time. By now, Jody was feeling like she had won over a major ally. In the ladies' room, though, another member of the team cornered her. What on Earth was she doing? Why was she publicly mocking the client? Jody was dumbfounded. She had been so wrapped up in herself she hadn't realized that the gentleman's winking wasn't, in fact, about her at all. It was a nervous tic.

Becoming fluent in body language is more essential than ever, especially now, when our face-to-face time with each other seems to be forever shrinking as we rely more heavily on electronic communication in the workplace and in our day-to-day lives. That means we have to glean as much as we possibly can from our personal encounters, because the unspoken cues people give in person can never be replicated in e-mails, text messages, or even phone calls. Over the phone, for example, you might easily assume that a prospective client's "Let me get back to you on that" means they want to devote more time to your proposal but need to take three other waiting calls. In person, though, the same words convey a different message when you see the client glancing away from you when uttering them: You're getting the brush-off, and had better react quickly if you want to save this deal. Dr. Lester Lefton has found in his studies of the workplace that a boss passing by someone's desk and giving them a pat on the back can provide an even greater morale boost than a formal letter of praise. "If I meet with my assistant and say, 'this is really important to me,' and tap my finger on the table, that's different than saying the same thing in an e-mail," Lefton says.

Likewise, what *isn't* said may, in effect, say it all. One of our favorite war stories from Madison Avenue is how Charlotte Beers, one of the pioneering women in advertising, won the Sears account. Back in the 1970s, Sears was all about power tools. As a woman, Charlotte felt at a distinct disadvantage pitching them. So five minutes into the crucial meeting with the Sears honchos, and without saying a word, Charlotte pulled out an electric drill, took it apart, and put it back together without so much as a dropped screw. Needless to say, she won the business. Show trumps tell.

Dating coach Rachel Greenwald, author of *Why He Didn't Call You Back,* says it's the tiny, barely perceptible things that can torpedo a potentially great date.

Rachel interviewed one thousand men to find out what it was that kept them from calling their dates back, and what she learned was that, in many cases, it wasn't a big thing that changed the mood, but a collection of small things.

"Often, a woman doesn't even realize that she's done something to turn him off," says Rachel. "A few little words or gestures during a first date can build up into a negative stereotype in a man's mind."

One man immediately dismissed a date who kept using

slang, like "that sucks," or "he's a brownnoser." He liked the woman otherwise, but quickly concluded her language would stop the relationship in its tracks: "I can't imagine ever introducing her to my boss," he explained.

Another man went out with a woman who told him he was loading the dishwasher incorrectly after she cooked dinner for him. This tiny comment, which she meant to be helpful, made him see her as too controlling. The solution, according to Rachel, is simple. "Constructive criticism doesn't belong anywhere on the first few dates," she says. "Save it for your employee performance reviews at work."

Making the other person feel important is a gift that Linda noticed Bill Clinton gave generously from the first time she met the former president while working on his advertising campaign in 1992.

"I was with a group of fifteen people. I was sure that he was talking directly to me through the entire hour and a half that we were with him. I was just so sure that it was *me*," Linda remembers. "Then I went over to someone else and that person said, 'He was talking to me the whole time.'"

If you watch Bill Clinton closely, though, the one thing you'll notice he does is to wait until he has come to the end of a sentence to shift his attention to another person. The result, which Linda experienced, is that "you absolutely believe that that entire sentence was meant for you."

You Have to Crack the Codes

The business world is all about cracking the codes. "As I like to say, 'Truths are couched politely, and rarely spoken directly,' " says Robin. "You quickly learn, for example, that someone emphasizing 'responsiveness' is a client who changes stuff every fifteen seconds and needs an agency that's not going to get flustered and can roll with the punches. So we look for clues: Are a client's sales bad because their message isn't right? Or is the ad working, and they just can't stand their agency?" When a company with a very successful commercial on the air called us to set up a meeting, we knew their current agency had a reputation in the industry for being arrogant and expensive. Since the ad was working, we deduced that the client's dissatisfaction was pretty much personal: They weren't being treated well. We took that cue and ran with it. Linda and Robin personally went to every meeting, no matter how minor. Members of our team made a point of frequently calling the prospective clients to share ideas or just chat. We knew we needed to send the signal that we were accessible, collaborative, and, yes, pleasant. We won the pitch. How you play the field is a matter of honing your intuition, and catching the myriad cues and clues that are out there.

Robin, as a native of the Bronx, is a Yankees fan by birthright; she believes baseball is a great case study for executive leadership:

Casual fans may think they're just enjoying a simple American pastime, but the serious fanatics know that players are constantly reading the tiniest of cues from both their teammates and their opponents. The CEO on the field is the catcher—the most strategic position on the team, and the only one who can see the entire field, both the batter and the defense. And one of the best catchers ever was

Yogi Berra. I had the honor of meeting the Yankee legend when he appeared in an Aflac commercial. Yogi was a great clue gatherer.

The beloved hall of famer recently shared with us some insights from his glory days in the fifties and sixties. "I studied the hitters a lot, you know," Yogi says. "When I played, we only had eight teams. You knew all the guys and everything. You knew what they hit." He studied his opponents not merely for their individual performances, but in relation to other players as well. He knew whose curveballs could strike out which hitter. He constantly watched the base runners for slight changes in body language that meant they were going to try to steal second, so he could signal the pitcher accordingly. He knew to watch the flags waving over the outfield for shifts in the wind that could affect how a ball would be hit. And because the catcher plays in virtually every game (unlike the rotating pitchers), he would know if a batter had changed his stance, or what kinds of pitches he was hitting the most. The pitcher relies on the catcher to know all these little details and send him signals on how to adjust his pitch. "I loved the game," Yogi explains. "I studied the game, you know?"

Studying the game you love makes you a formidable opponent, and when you're on the lookout for every little cue and clue on the field and off, you set yourself up for one great hit after another.

Or, as Yogi himself is fond of saying, "You can observe a lot just by watching."

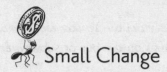

Small Change

PUT YOURSELF ON INSTANT REPLAY. Videotape your next presentation, or even a staff meeting. Then watch yourself specifically to see what nonverbal cues you send to others. Are you constantly looking down at your notes when someone else is speaking? If so, you may as well just hold up a sign saying, "Bored. Waiting for my turn."

ENLIST A FRIENDLY CRITIC. Have a colleague or business partner give you the hard answers to some tough questions: Do I give off any negative vibes? Do I have any signature phrases, gestures, or tics? What bad habits do I display in meetings or during presentations?

BE A DIPLOMAT. Henry Kissinger, the former secretary of state under Richard Nixon, was famous for being able to work a party of five hundred people and say something personal to each guest. He wasn't a human Wikipedia. The trick was to memorize just one thing about each person he met. It can be innocuous, like where someone's daughter is attending college, or whether the husband plays golf. Look through your appointment calendar and make a list of five people you're scheduled to meet with in the coming week. Now find out one casual bit of information about each person and commit it to memory. Drop it into your next conversation. Or if you've met the person before, jot down a salient fact or detail or two in your Outlook address file.

LOSE THE SOUNDTRACK. Try a little sensory-deprivation experiment. Try wearing earplugs on the bus or subway, and see what you notice about the other passengers. What are they "saying" without words? The next time you're in a meeting, try to imagine, for a few moments, what it would be like if you could hit the "mute" button. Notice the little cues, like how people place themselves around the conference table, or whether someone is smiling with just their mouth, or their whole face. Is the guy next to you who's fiddling incessantly with his pen simply nervous, or terminally bored? Such cues speak volumes.

Chapter 7

Little Mistakes
Spell Disaster

If you think small things don't matter, try spending the night in a room with a mosquito.
—The Dalai Lama

Elvin Bale was considered the greatest circus daredevil of his time, a Ringling Bros. aerialist so fearless that Evel Knievel once shook his hand and told him he was crazy. The child of a tiger tamer, Elvin had grown up in the circus; it was in his blood, and he couldn't imagine ever leaving it. He became a solo trapeze star at seventeen and spent his career designing and perfecting new acts, always upping the ante to give the cheering crowds a fresh thrill. He rode a motorcycle blindfolded across a high-wire and performed stunts as he raced around a giant, spinning "Wheel of Death."

Of all the daring tricks in Bale's repertoire, the safest was the act he called the Human Space Shuttle, where Elvin was shot out of a giant cannon to fly like a superhero across the big top before landing on an air bag on the other side. He owned the cannon—and the act—and could practically do the routine in his sleep. But one day, in 1987, while performing at a Hong Kong theme park, Elvin Bale made a small mistake.

Despite the illusion and the deafening boom it makes when fired, a circus cannon is not a gun: it's all hydraulics and sound effects. It functions like an oversized piston. In rehearsals, sandbag dummies are used to calculate how much force is needed to carry its human projectile how far. The dummy must weigh exactly the same, of course, as Bale, the human cannonball. However, on that fateful day in Hong Kong, something went wrong. The sandbag facsimile of Elvin Bale had been left outside on rain-soaked ground. Bale had noticed the wet pavement and felt the bag to make sure it was dry before he went to use it for his test shot. And it felt okay. But Bale neglected to weigh it to double-check. He didn't realize that some of the sand inside was still damp, making the dummy heavier than usual. He set his usual calibrations for that day's performance, based on the dummy. It wasn't until he was in mid-flight that Bale sensed something was drastically wrong: He was flying faster, and farther, than he was supposed to. He saw the air cushion he was supposed to land on sail past him below as he overshot his mark.

One tiny mistake was about to cost him everything he held dear.

Elvin remained calm, feeling as if it were all happening in slow motion. Maybe, he thought, if he made a small adjustment—if he rotated his body, he might land on his feet instead of on his back, as he usually did with his cushioned back flop. It was his only chance to survive the landing. Making the subtle adjustment, he slammed feet first into the concrete floor, shattering both ankles, a knee, a leg, and his spine. The world's greatest circus daredevil, at age forty-one, was left paralyzed from the waist down.

His horrific accident is testament to what can happen when the power of small is overlooked. In truth, near misses happen every day, in every line of work. And while our lives are rarely at risk, our careers may well be.

Hats Off

One of Linda's most unforgettable—and sobering—gaffes happened years ago, when she was the executive creative director at another ad agency. Toys "R" Us was an important account. Generations of children had grown up with Linda's infectious "I don't wanna grow up, I'm a Toys "R" Us Kid" jingle ingrained in their memories. Linda had established a strong relationship with Toys "R" Us over the years and had produced hundreds of commercials for them. You would think that making a toy commercial would be child's play. But that didn't prevent a near disaster.

The assignment itself was hardly daunting: Toys "R" Us needed a promotional television spot to let customers know about an upcoming sale. What they wanted to communicate to consumers was a sense of fun, excitement, great value, and urgency, so that customers would take advantage of this limited-time offer. Linda's creative team came up with a humorous idea to use kids pretending to be soldiers mustering their troops for the big event.

There was the usual choreographed chaos on the day of the shoot—scripts to double-check, props to organize, harried assistants and assistants-to-the-assistant scurrying about, production crews setting up, wardrobe stylists wriggling child actors into costumes. All of the kids would be wearing a military hat of some kind—an admiral's cap, army helmet, or such—like a big game of dress-up. Linda wasn't at the shoot herself but was assured by the creative team that everything had run smoothly, and she signed off on the final edit. The commercial went on the air.

And then came the phone call.

A spokesman for a powerful watchdog group was on the other line, outraged, demanding the commercial be taken off the air immediately. Linda was both alarmed and dumbfounded. What was the problem?

It turned out that one of the young actors in the television spot, an African-American child, was wearing a play Confederate soldier's cap. To make matters worse, he had been saluting along with all the other kid "soldiers." He was on the screen for less than a second—it took a freeze-frame to identify the cap. But there it was, and now this influential watchdog group was on the phone, demanding to know why we were trying to make a mockery of one of the most painful chapters of American history. Of course we weren't, and Linda was beyond mortified. She sought to assure them that this was an oversight, a phenomenally stupid mistake.

While the wardrobe stylist may have been the one to actually put that particular hat on that particular child, Linda to this day blames herself for not catching it. "I should have been more attentive," she laments. "Even thinking about it now makes my stomach churn." What seemed like no big deal—pulling hats from a prop bag and plopping them on kids' heads—turned out to be a very big deal indeed. Reputations, businesses, and careers were on the line. In the end, the offending scene was immediately cut from the commercial. After the company apologized profusely to the organization, and to Toys "R" Us, the entire team was enrolled in a diversity training workshop to ensure that such an oversight did not happen again. Linda found the process so worthwhile that it became a permanent part of KTG's training. In fact, our diversity trainer, Kendal Wright, gave us the motto we've embraced at our company ever since about the importance of paying close attention to the smallest details: "What you ignore becomes more."

We're all human. We all make mistakes. Some are laughable, others lamentable. But by their very definition, mistakes are avoidable. Perfection may be impossible, but what a difference it can make in your career and your life if you fine-tune your focus enough to avoid even some of those mistakes. It's easy to brush aside the little things, to tell yourself they don't really matter. But ask yourself if you would have the same cavalier attitude about the surgeon repairing your husband's heart valve, the accountant preparing your tax returns, or the soloist performing at your daughter's wedding?

Sometimes forgetting to take care of the smallest details can have the biggest repercussions. It's a lesson the Air Force had to reinforce in its ranks after a stealth fighter plane crashed during an air show in Baltimore because four inexpensive bolts were missing from one wing. The pilot ejected safely, and no one on the ground was hurt, but the $42 million F-117 was lost.

Robin's own airspace was invaded several years ago as she was getting ready to go on vacation:

A week before the trip my refrigerator broke down. The repairman came, jiggled some wires and got it running, but cautioned that it was just a temporary fix—what was really needed was a small, inexpensive replacement part. He urged me to set up another appointment so he could order the part and return to install it. But that task slipped my mind as I spent the next few days getting things squared away at the office. When we returned from vacation, we opened the door and were nearly bowled over by the odor of decay. The refrigerator must have broken down shortly after we left. The entire contents, including a freezerful of chicken breasts and hamburger patties, had been rotting for weeks. Now I know why detectives on crime shows cover their noses when they enter a murder scene. The smell was so intense it had permeated the entire first floor of our home. We not only had to pay to have the offending appliance hauled away and purchase a new one, we had to have the entire house cleaned to get rid of the smell. What originally would have cost less than a hundred dollars ended up costing thousands, and the memory of that putrid odor will never quite fade away.

Be Letter Perfect

Needless to say, at KTG both of us have become zealots about everything from double-checking the decimals in our checkbooks to proofreading each and every document that we print, display, or digitally deliver to our clients. It may seem picayune and obsessive to focus so much attention on minor details like spelling and typos. There are always more pressing matters on the agenda. But think how you felt the last time someone mangled the pronunciation of your last name, got your title or some other personal detail wrong, or introduced you incorrectly to a group at a party. No matter what else follows, it's hard to put aside that small detail that virtually screams, "Hey, you're not important enough for me to remember who you are."

Even the tiniest error can impact your future, as Linda recollects from her college days:

I was dating a brilliant premed student, Paul, in my senior year. With a string of straight As, Paul was certain he would have an array of outstanding medical schools to choose from. But to his chagrin, he was rejected from all of them. Paul was confused and bitterly disappointed. He had laboriously filed every application form, had excellent references, and had spent weeks toiling over his required essay, detailing his passionate desire to become a doctor.

After the final rejection letter, Paul allowed me to read the essay he had sent to the admission boards. And there it was, the mistake that cost him his lifelong dream: he had spelled the word "medicine" m-e-d-e-c-i-n-e. Just under the wire, Paul applied to one more school and was accepted. It was a last minute remedy to an unfortunate oversight, but hopefully one that has allowed Paul to cure a great many patients in his medical career.

With the pace of business today, managing the avalanche of details while working at lightning speed is difficult. But when both money and emotions can be conveyed with the tap of a finger, taking care of the little things is more crucial than ever. Media expert and author Michael Levine calls it the broken-window effect. Fail to fix the little things, and before you know it, the whole neighborhood is sliding into neglect and disrepair. The solution? Absolute vigilance. "If you notice that the carpet on the floor at your dentist's office is a little worn, you might find yourself wondering whether the dental instruments have been replaced recently," Levine writes in his book *Broken Windows, Broken Business*. "In business, perception is even more critical. The way a customer (or potential customer) *perceives* your business is a crucial element in your success or failure. Make one mistake, have even one rude employee, let that customer walk away with a negative experience *one time*, and you are inviting disaster."

Don't Get Your Wires Crossed

Our industry, the advertising industry, is rife with famous blunders, which live on in perpetuity thanks to popular blooper sites on the Internet. In Mexico, a ballpoint pen ad for Parker Pen was supposed to promise that it wouldn't leak in your pocket and embarrass you. But the company used the Spanish verb *embarazar*, which *sounds* like it should mean "to embarrass," but—embarrassingly enough—doesn't. Which is why the Spanish ads boasted: "It won't leak in your pocket and get you pregnant." In Brazil, Portuguese slang was the undoing of Ford when it belatedly discovered that the word "Pinto" referred to tiny male genitals. A friend of ours who was delivering a presentation to French cereal executives in Paris memorably described cornflakes "without condoms" (*sans preservatifs*) rather than without preservatives.

One of the most famous stories in the annals of American journalism happened back in 1933, when the Associated Press still relied on teletype machines to send news to newspapers around the world. Late-breaking sports results were the particular bane of editors and typesetters.

That year, in the small town of Walsenburg, Colorado, a new guy was handling the wires at the *World-Independent Newspaper* on the day of the Indy 500, and he had deadline jitters about getting the race results before the presses started running. There was no live radio coverage of the race to monitor and, of course, there was no television coverage yet. The nervous newbie in Colorado was scared to death that the AP's bulletin wouldn't arrive in time for his deadline. The AP offered to have a newsman telegraph the results—known as "sending it overhead"—the moment the race ended. The wire service relayed this promise to the *World-Independent* via teletype:

WILL OVERHEAD WINNER OF INDY 500.

The anxious Colorado editor immediately slapped a banner headline into the edition heading to press:

OVERHEAD WINS INDIANAPOLIS RACE.

He quickly cobbled together a few grafs to top the background material, explaining how an unknown racer named Will Overhead had pulled a stunning come-from-behind upset to win the famous race.

The blooper itself made news, and the gaffe was recounted in journalism textbooks for decades to come. The town of Walsenburg capitalized on its notoriety with good humor, celebrating the mistake with an annual Will Overhead Day and parade.

And the following year, the AP sent a tongue-in-cheek advisory across the wire:

EDITORS NOTE: WILL OVERHEAD NOT ENTERED IN KENTUCKY DERBY.

Sometimes having the good grace to laugh at yourself is all you can do. Intentional or not, mistakes are sometimes all that anyone remembers, whether it's a comma misplaced in a budget proposal, or Chief Justice Roberts misplacing the word "faithfully" while administering the presidential oath of office. (A "supreme" error on his part.)

Be Fool-Proof

At work, the first line of defense against embarrassing mistakes is to build a strong support team, with accountability as the guiding principle. There is no shortage of costly management consultants or academic tomes waiting to tell you how to hire the right people, of course. But Zappos, the wildly successful Internet shoe outlet, has found a nearly foolproof way to weed out bad apples before it's too late: The company actually bribes people to fire themselves. A week or so into the intense four-week training program for new hires, Zappos offers a thousand-dollar bonus to anyone who wants to quit immediately. The philosophy behind CEO Tony Hsieh's unusual strategy? Anyone willing to accept the offer clearly doesn't have the sense of commitment Zappos expects, and it's far cheaper to pay for the hiring mistake immediately and move on. That strikes us as a creative and cost-effective insurance policy when it comes to safeguarding your corporate reputation and culture.

Sometimes, however, we become so consumed with avoiding the big mistakes, we forget to read the fine print that could literally save our lives. Gene Simmons, mega rock star and founder of the band Kiss, told us about a moment in his career when he was so obsessed with the machinations of spitting flames out of his mouth, he never bothered to heed the warning on the can of hairspray he was using. "I emerged from the fog in full Kiss gear, carrying a sword with the hilt lit on fire and my mouth full of kerosene. I came to center stage and I spit out the kerosene. A huge ball of fire erupted out of my mouth, and the audience went nuts. It was then that I smelled something burning." His hair had burst into flames, as a result of the flammable hairspray. "Even though it had directions and warnings on the spray can, it didn't specifically say, 'Gene, I know you're in Kiss and I know you're gonna spit fire, so please don't use this!' You have to sort of apply the rules and the warning signs of life to how they affect you. That's in business and anything else."

But probably the best way to prevent disaster is to simply trust that small voice within each and every one of us. That sense of intuition has saved us time and again from making mistakes both big and small.

Robin recalls the time she was interviewing a highly

qualified candidate for a senior position at the agency. The woman looked fabulous on paper, and had all the right answers to the usual interview questions. She seemed like the perfect candidate. But something about her hyperenthusiasm seemed off—more than just job interview jitters—and I couldn't quite put my finger on it. So I excused myself and went down the hall to Linda's office. "I just want you to go introduce yourself," I said. Linda popped into Robin's office, chatted with the applicant for a few minutes, then returned to her own office, where Robin was waiting. Linda shut the door and delivered her verdict: "She's crazy." Robin nodded in agreement. We never did find out whether the woman was overcaffeinated or undermedicated, but we hired someone else, and the stories we later heard about our near hire from other firms validated our gut reaction.

Of course, genuine perfection is an illusion, an impossible standard to meet. In fact, showing a little humility and vulnerability makes us appear human, endearing us to others in ways that bravado never can. Still, we live in a competitive world where we feel pressure to hide our imperfections and "fake it till you make it." We're afraid to let any gaps in our knowledge show. Sometimes, though, what those gaps expose isn't a lack of knowledge, but a wealth of character.

Don't Be Afraid to Ask

Within days of his graduation from the University of Michigan, Randall Tallerico was on his way to the big leagues with a job at Robert Solomon and Associates, one of the top advertising agencies in Detroit.

Randall had been in his cubicle for less than a week when he was summoned by the creative director, Kathleen Hay. Kathleen sat behind her desk, imposing and beautiful, with coffee in one hand, a cigarette in the other, and the phone tucked under her ear as she issued orders to a stream of people madly rushing in and out of her office.

Randall approached uncertainly, like an obedient schoolboy. Kathleen distractedly waved a piece of paper at him. Randall's eyes lit up: his first big assignment, straight from the boss herself.

"Here," she said. "Schlep this to production."

She gave Randall the layout for an ad. Randall was a fresh-faced farm boy from the Midwest who wouldn't have known a latke from a kugel if it smacked him in the schnoz. He had no idea what "schlep" meant. He waited a moment for further instructions, but Kathleen had already turned her attention to someone else. With a polite "yes, ma'am," Randall retreated to his cubicle and proceeded to have a very quiet nervous breakdown. He was about to choke his first time at bat.

"It probably means to xerox it," he thought. "Or to reduce it." So he quickly did some research. He checked his marketing books. Nothing on schlep. He checked his advertising books. Still nothing. Asking a colleague would only prove how ignorant he was. And Google? Sorry, not invented yet.

How was he going to face his formidable boss and admit he didn't know how to "schlep"? He would surely be fired.

I'm going to have to go to law school, he thought. *My career is over.*

After two hours of agonizing, Randall pulled himself together, steeled himself for the inevitable, and walked into Kathleen's office, which was filled with the cigarette smoke and noisy arguments of advertising execs hammering out a client presentation.

Randall cleared his throat.

"Excuse me, ma'am."

Nobody heard him.

"Ma'am?"

"What do you want, kid?" the creative director barked when she finally noticed the young man in the big horn-rimmed glasses hovering nervously in front of her.

"I—I—I don't know what it means to schlep."

And just as Randall had feared, the boss began to laugh so hard she had to put her coffee down. Still roaring, she dialed Robert Solomon, the head of the company, no doubt to tell him what an idiot their new hire was. Randall was petrified when Solomon himself stepped into the office.

This is it, he thought.

"Robert," the creative director announced, "the new kid doesn't know what 'schlep' means."

Robert Solomon shook with laughter, and Randall shrank down even smaller in his new Brooks Brothers suit.

"Kid," said Kathleen, at long last. "It's Yiddish. It means to bring. Just bring it to production. And don't worry, you're gonna do great here. It's good to speak up when you don't know the answer."

Randall did do very well at the agency. He soon received a raise and a promotion, along with a gift from the big boss, a copy of the book *The Joys of Yiddish*.

Randall learned a humbling but important lesson that day. He turned a near disaster into the moment that forever endeared him to his bosses. He distinguished himself within his company by never being intimidated by what he didn't know, and having the courage and common sense to just ask, instead.

Asking questions, no matter how seemingly dumb or trivial, is the smart way to address and solve problems when they're still small and manageable. No one can be expected to have all the answers to everything. As the Chinese proverb says, "He who asks a question is a fool for five minutes; he who does not remains a fool forever."

Learning to let go of our pride and to ask for help, for another set of eyes or ears, is critical in avoiding the little disasters that can undo our best intentions (and weeks of hard work). And this is true whether you're the boss or the newest, youngest, most junior hire.

Psychologist, professor, and author Carol Dweck spent more than two decades studying why some people realize their potential while others who are just as talented fall short. The answer, she found, wasn't in natural ability, but in perception. In her book *Mindset: The New Psychology of Success*, the professor divides people into those with a fixed mindset and those with a growth mindset. If you have a fixed mindset, you believe that talents and abilities are something you either have or don't, and you're doomed to a lifetime of trying to prove yourself over and over in order to look smart and talented at all costs. Mistakes are crippling. But for those with a growth mindset, the sky is the limit, because such people believe that talents can be cultivated and that great abilities flourish over time. Mistakes are more likely to be grasped as a chance to learn and improve.

Stay in the Moment

Falling down is a part of life. Robin, an avid figure skater, has faced that cold, hard reality plenty of times on the ice: Falling down is inevitable. She knows that the real art—the sign of a true champion—is in how quickly and gracefully you get back up.

Every skater is told to "stay in your program." Whether it's on the ice in front of an international television audience in the millions or in a corner office in front of no one but your boss, when you fall, you need to focus your mind to immediately get back in your program and stay in the present. Forget what just happened: You need to immediately be thinking about the move you are supposed to be doing right now. Skaters know that once you finish a move, jump, or spin, it's over—whether you executed it perfectly or not. Coaches instill this in even their youngest gold-medal dreamers: Even if you do not fully land the jump, you still finish in an ending position, as if to say . . . that's over, move on. Everything about skating is staying in the moment and knowing where your mind and body are RIGHT NOW.

Staying in the moment—being acutely aware of where you are and what you are doing—doesn't happen serendipitously. Every mother who has taken a small child to a swimming pool has experienced it firsthand, but learning to stay in the moment in situations that aren't potentially life-or-death takes a more conscious effort. It takes practice. At KTG, we're obsessive about it. Before any presentation, we insist that our employees rehearse their material over and over so they can be fully present when the big moment arrives. A presentation is its own production: You need to coordinate who stands where, who cues for audio, who holds the storyboards, who delivers which lines. And until you rehearse, you can't anticipate the little things that might go wrong. You discover where the timing is off, or where the joke needs to be. You work out all the kinks.

When we were gearing up to pitch Revlon, we pulled a typical all-nighter to practice our big presentation. There were more than a hundred props to keep track of, from eyeliner pencils and mascara wands to a row of office chairs arranged to look like an airline cabin. We choreographed it down to the second. The session dragged on for hours, deep into the night, the empty pizza boxes and potato chip bags piling up until the cleaning lady gave us a choice: Either we cleared out so she could vacuum, or we could make our big pitch in a conference room that now looked and smelled like Animal House. With the presentation just a few hours away, we finally packed it in. But the mistakes we avoided by focusing so intently on the smallest details were well worth the sleep lost. And we won the account. That kind of rehearsal, whether we're arranging the details of a date with someone we care about or preparing for a sales call at work, is critical. Practicing what we are going to say, and how we are going to say it, helps enormously to get your points across in the way you intended—whether you are talking to your son's teacher or making a presentation to your colleagues or boss. And remember, whether you have a big part or a small one—even the tiniest oversight can ruin the entire production. It's terrific advice we found reinforced in a pretty unlikely place for two girls from the Bronx: the summit of Mount Everest.

Check Your Baggage

We were thrilled to get a chance to work with Canadian explorer Jamie Clarke, who had signed on to do a campaign with our client, Champion sportswear. Clarke has conquered six of the world's seven tallest peaks, including Everest, which he's in training to attempt again. He told us his checklist for a major expedition such as Everest is as thick as the white pages for a city of a million people. Each person on the climb is responsible for five hundred or more items. "It's the tiny things that can creep up and get complicated and go wrong," Clarke told us.

One time he and his partner were trekking high in the Canadian Rockies, only to discover fourteen hours into their climb that they had forgotten an eighty-nine-cent lighter. They needed the lighter to light their camp stove. The stove was their only means of melting snow to obtain drinking water, which climbers go through quickly at high altitudes under such rigorous conditions. Dehydration is swift and lethal. Clarke and his partner were forced to turn back. "People die with that piece of equipment being lost—an eighty-nine-cent lighter."

While you may not be ready to load up a yak, hire a sherpa, and attempt an assault on the world's highest peak, the lessons of mountaineering offer a useful metaphor for life.

Obtaining superior results, whether climbing a Himalayan peak or hoping to make your way up a corporate org chart, comes about from paying close attention to everyday details, planning ahead, and being committed every step of the way. When you do, you'll be amazed at what you can accomplish.

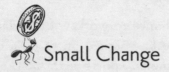 Small Change

BE PROOF POSITIVE. Learn to proofread the details in your personal and professional life like a copy editor. Don't just rely on spell check—or someone or something else to bail you out. Read your speech, report, or business correspondence out loud. It's the only surefire way to catch an error.

QUESTION YOURSELF. At work, when you have a new task or project, jot down five questions about the assignment. Can you answer every one? Make yourself a cheat sheet before you dive in, with the names, phone numbers, and e-mail addresses of people with information you're likely to need. Keep your cheat sheet handy.

TEACH, DON'T PREACH. We all learn through our mistakes. True leaders have the confidence and courage to share those hard-earned lessons with their staff. With those under you, make it clear that what you expect isn't perfection, but accountability. At staff meetings, or with a colleague or team member who's struggling, share a story or two about mistakes you made along the way in your career, and what you learned from them.

Chapter 8
Make It Big by Thinking Small

The real voyage of discovery consists not in seeking new land-
scapes but in having new eyes.
—Marcel Proust

We're often told to think big, to see the larger picture, to
not lose sight of the forest for the trees. In creating a business, however, some of the best, and freshest, ideas come
from often overlooked, and insignificant, places.

After a divorce that left her more than a million dollars in debt from a real-estate venture, Carol Gardner was
fifty-two years old with no job, no income, and no prospects. She was understandably depressed. "My attorney
just shook her head and said, 'you need to get a therapist
or get a dog,' " she recalls. The rueful quip actually made a
certain sense, though. "Love and laughter are what I need
in my life," Gardner reasoned. A dog would provide both
without the insurance hassles or the fifty-minute clock.

Gardner had always admired bulldogs, and when she
heard of a four-month-old pup named Zelda whose owners were giving her up because they had lost interest in
possibly breeding her, Gardner went to have a look. "As
soon as I walked in, her face was just a mirror image of

how I felt in my heart. She needed love, and I needed love."

What she needed more immediately, however, was a good supply of puppy chow for her new companion. With that objective in mind, Gardner decided to enter a local pet store's annual Christmas card contest. The prize was forty pounds of dog food a month for an entire year. "Okay, Zelda, you get twenty pounds and I get twenty pounds, and with ketchup maybe it's not so bad," Gardner joked as she plopped a Santa hat on the pooch's head and put her in a bubble bath, using the suds to fashion Zelda a flowing beard. She sent off her photo of Zelda Claus with a zinger of a caption: "For Christmas, I got a dog for my husband . . . good trade, huh?" She won the contest, and Gardner turned the winning photo into a holiday card for friends that year. Their delight in the little dog—her ugly-mug muse—mirrored Gardner's own. "Oh my God, there's a Zelda in all of us," she realized.

The success of that holiday card gave Gardner an inspiration. "The lightbulb went on," Gardner says. What if she turned Zelda into a line of funny greeting cards? She visited the card shop and sized up the potential competition. In fact, there was none. "No one had taken a live dog, given it a name, and designed cards around it. I saw an opportunity. It was different, and it was daring." And with a seven-figure debt looming over her, she surely had nothing more to lose.

Gardner had once been a creative director in advertising, and she knew when a model had that "it" factor. Zelda had it in spades. Gardner called the best professional photographer she knew and asked him to come shoot some frames on spec. "You mean you're dressing up your dog, you want me to come over and take pictures, and you can't pay me?" he repeated, just to be sure he had heard her right. "Yes," Gardner replied. "Just trust me." Her conviction won him over, and it also soon convinced a printer to extend Gardner credit for ninety days so she could run off her first sample batch of cards. Each card would feature Zelda in comical outfits, offering a snippet of advice, such as, "Go braless . . . it pulls the wrinkles down!" Gardner dubbed her fledgling company Zelda Wisdom, and it wasn't long before Hallmark took notice of the quirky cards, turning one woman's whimsical notion—borne out of sheer desperation—into an international line of greeting cards, gifts, clothing, jewelry, and inspirational books.

Zelda is a teenager now, a full-fledged diva with two understudies and appearance contracts that demand first-class travel and luxury accommodations. Gardner shares the wisdom Zelda hasn't put on a card yet, the philosophy that turned her own life around: "You have to take stock of who you are and what you love, and follow your intuition," Gardner advises.

Over and over we have found that the ideas in business that really soar often come from a small flight of fancy. Perhaps that's because so many of the barriers are removed when you think that something doesn't really matter and the pressure is off. Carol Gardner had nothing to lose by taking funny pictures of her dog. Being too tied up in a problem or too invested in a way of thinking often inhibits us from discovering that next big idea. That's because some of the biggest ideas start very small. Pressure fuels defeat and failure. You may not need to invest years of research, an army of employees, or vast resources to find the next new thing.

Sometimes, like Zelda, it's right there sleeping at your feet.

Find Your Niche

Entrepreneur magazine reports that niche businesses are growing at a rate of 20 to 25 percent a year. Many of these businesses target a small segment of a market that has either been overlooked entirely or is being underserved. Niche businesses are often ideal for would-be entrepreneurs, since they can be launched on a modest scale and by definition have little or no direct competition. And if the invention or service resonates with consumers, that niche endeavor can quickly become a very successful product or store or even create a whole new business category. In 2007 alone, the U.S. patent office issued over 180,000 new patents, roughly one every three mintues. And some of those patents include new twists on existing ideas or, as in Leslie Blodgett's case, an idea that is literally *ages* old—mineral makeup.

Cleopatra and her ancient Egyptian girlfriends may have worn it first, but two thousand years later, in 1997, Blodgett put a whole new spin on having an "earthy" natural glow. Her company, Bare Escentuals, started as a tiny San Francisco beauty boutique. One of their exclusive products was a unique facial foundation. Unlike most foundation products, which feel heavy and laden with preservatives, bareMinerals was a powder made from crushed, natural minerals. It was 100 percent pure, contained no preservatives, and carried the claim "so gentle you could even sleep in it." With a bit of marketing bravado, Leslie convinced the QVC shopping network to give her an appearance on their channel. In just six minutes, bareMinerals went from niche to notorious. Today it is a $500 million plus brand sold on TV, online, and in 750 Sephora beauty stores around the world and has inspired an entire category of mineral makeup entries from L'Oréal, CoverGirl, and Revlon.

Sometimes implementing a brilliant idea is as simple as taking an old message and putting it in a new location. That was the genius behind the Wizmark talking urinal. The men's room of a bar is the last stop many patrons make before heading home. The Wizmark urinal "senses" when someone approaches to use the urinal, and plays a prerecorded message reminding him to flag a cab or call a friend to take him home if he's had a few too many. The product has attracted media attention around the world and installations have been funded by seven states around the country. Massachusetts has placed them in Fenway Park, the home of the Boston Red Sox and beer consumption by the barrelful. And in a true example of poetic justice, New York's Nassau County has funded the installation of these drinking and driving deterrents via the fines paid by convicted DWI offenders.

There are an infinite number of successful business ideas just waiting to be born. Sometimes all you need is a little sparkle to bring one to life.

Add a Little Glitter

Sheri Schmelzer was just playing with her three kids when she decided to decorate her children's colorful old pairs of Crocs. Pulling out her sewing kit, Schmelzer started plugging the signature holes in the popular resin clogs with buttons and rhinestones. Her seven-year-old daughter was ecstatic. Each of the family's dozen pairs of Crocs were soon sporting their own unique charms. The comments they inevitably drew in public convinced Sheri she must be on to something. Next thing she knew, Sheri had a booming business going in her basement, designing and making the charms she dubbed Jibbitz. She found manufacturers in China and production skyrocketed. The headquarters for Crocs happened to be just a few miles away in their hometown of Boulder, Colorado. When one of the company founders spotted one of the Schmelzer children in her blinged-out clogs, he handed her a business card and told her to have her mommy get in touch. A year after Sheri Schmelzer first rummaged around in her sewing kit that fateful afternoon, Crocs bought her niche business for $20 million.

Sometimes adding a little sparkle or an extra twist to products and services we use every day can result in wildly successful businesses. And that special twist can be as simple as a name change, the California Prune Board discovered. The name "prune" carries a lot of geriatric and medicinal baggage in many people's minds—resulting in sagging sales with younger consumers. When research revealed that referring to the fruit as a "dried plum" made it sound a lot more delectable to nine out of ten people, the Food and Drug Administration gave the board permission to officially change the name of their product. The result? A very "plum" turnover in sales.

Let an Irritation Be Your Inspiration

We all have pet peeves. But how many of us are willing to invest the creative energy into finding a pragmatic solution, rather than complaining about the problem?

As the mother of newborn twin girls, Jen Groover found herself longing for a bit of order in a life turned suddenly chaotic. At the grocery store one night, the Pennsylvania mom had the same thought as every woman who's kept a line of annoyed shoppers waiting while she fumbles through a cluttered purse for coupons, change, or a credit card: Why can't someone come up with a better handbag?

Later that evening, Groover was unloading her dishwasher when she had what she would later call her "a-ha moment." Would a dishwasher silverware caddy work as a purse organizer? She popped it into an empty diaper bag, and was so pleased by the result that she began carrying it around and showing it off to friends. They raved. Realizing she was on to something, Groover patented the idea, lined up a manufacturer, and launched her product, which she called the Butler Bag. Within a couple of years, Groover had become a wildly successful entrepreneur with a major licensing deal, a calendar full of TV appearances and speaking engagements, and a host of new products in development.

Before the Internet shrank the international market-place to a global village, the Jen Groovers of the world would have needed cash, clout, and the connections of a major backer behind them before they could even produce a prototype of their design or innovation.

Today, all it takes to launch a business is the ability to see opportunities that others have missed—by harnessing the power of thinking small. The playing field is more level than ever. You don't need the backing of a major corporation to make your idea profitable—all you need is a laptop. Check out InnoCentive, at innocentive.com (the name is a combination of "innovation" and "incentive") and compete to solve problems that existing companies have posted on-line. All the ideas are legally protected and kept confidential, but the best idea can win up to $100,000. No problem is too small to result in a potentially profitable solution. Swiss-born Ambros Huggin received a $20,000 prize for finding a way to keep yogurt cultures longer. The bottom line: If a problem matters to you, it will almost certainly matter to others as well. All you need is the inspiration, perspiration, and dedication to find a solution.

But too often, the temptation to overthink solutions is what leads to $640 government toilet seats and screwdrivers that cost as much as a plane ticket. Sometimes it makes sense to forget focus groups, endless research, and sophisticated business plans, and simply think how a child might solve the vexing problem at hand. The trouble with the way we think and look at things as adults, however, is that our brains are overloaded with a distracting array of assumptions and specialized information that stymie our ability to make the leap that leads to new discoveries. While well-funded research and development teams were spending millions of dollars finding ways to design "smart kitchens" for futuristic space stations, a four-year-old Houston girl was busy solving her own problem. In the process, she became the youngest person ever granted a patent from the U.S. Patent and Trademark Office. What she invented was a suction-cup device to help open high cupboards with round knobs. We have to applaud her ingenuity, and hope she finally reached that candy stash!

The four-year-old knew instinctively what plenty of adults with MBAs still haven't figured out: The first key to success is pinpointing exactly what the underlying problem is. Even if that problem is as basic as picking a place to eat.

Fill a Need

Tim and Nina Zagat were Ivy League lawyers who appreciated good food. One evening in 1979, the Zagats were dining out with friends in New York City. They had read glowing reviews of the restaurant beforehand, but the meal turned out to be disappointing. The Zagats and their guests wondered how the reviewers could have been so off base. Tim suggested the group start noting the pluses and minuses of their own dining experiences at various restaurants, then ask their friends and business acquaintances to do the same. He would compile their reviews, and they would all benefit from a full and fair analysis of a restaurant's food, ambience, and pricing. It seemed like a nice, fun way for everyone to share useful information.

The first compilation of those informal surveys was

written on both sides of a single sheet of paper torn from a legal pad and handed out to friends. More friends and more reviews led to a regular newsletter, which soon begged to be turned into a booklet.

Despite the survey's grassroots popularity, though, the Zagats were initially rebuffed when they tried to publish their findings. But they didn't want to stop doing what they loved, so they started printing guidebooks on their own. When bookstores began getting orders for more, the Zagats quickly realized that their little hobby could spawn a big business.

Today, that small glimmer of an idea over a noisy dinner table has become a global enterprise. Zagat Guides sells 5.5 million copies in one hundred countries, with over 300,000 reviewers contributing to the popular, often witty surveys, which have expanded to include ratings of hotels and even golf courses.

The Zagats didn't invent restaurant reviews, obviously. But they *reinvented* them.

And, in the process, they were among the first entrepreneurs to build a business based on consumer input. As Nina Zagat points out, "Long before the phrase 'user-generated content' existed, we had a vision that the best way to get people the information they needed was from other people, and not from professional critics." Moreover, you don't have to pay those consumers a dime!

Find Your Sweet Spot

"I'm often asked, 'Why would you give up a promising career in law to bake cakes?' " Warren Brown says, laughing. Some people still think he's crazy, but most, he insists, "totally understand what I've done."

After graduating from George Washington University in 1998 with a law degree and a master's in public health, Brown achieved his goal of becoming an attorney and began litigating health-care fraud for the federal government. Although Brown's career was on the rise, he began to realize it wasn't enough to measure achievement by how big or prestigious his job was. Or how large the paycheck.

What made his heart race was something more humble—an eight-inch layer-cake pan. He remembers one beautiful fall morning in 1999 when he was taking a shuttle flight from D.C. to New York to spend a weekend in the city with family members. Brown had always enjoyed baking—it was fun, interesting, and, most of all, deeply satisfying. Warren Brown was the guy who always showed up with a delicious homemade cake, and afterward there was never a crumb left. For the trip, he had made a simple chocolate layer cake. Brown put it on a white dinner plate and covered it with plastic wrap before setting off to New York. To his surprise, seemingly everyone along the way noticed the cake and had something to say about it—from airport security guards to flight attendants to fellow passengers.

"As I sat at the passenger pickup waiting for my aunt Yvette and her friend Kim," Brown recounts on his popular website, "I just stared into space thinking about what just happened. Why was everyone so excited? After a few moments, I realized that I was staring right at my future: scratch-made cake. Its strong appeal meant potential. Right then and there I decided that I would start a cake business."

He opened a tiny bakery called CakeLove in the nation's capital in 2002. The original shop has since spawned four suburban branches, and Brown has become a household name with his *Sugar Rush* show on the Food Network and his acclaimed cookbook on the art of baking cakes.

"When I changed careers, I realized that baking is hard, messy work," he says. "But even though my bones and joints often ache and my mind becomes dizzyingly tired at the end of each day, baking lifts my spirits and rewards me in many ways. One of the best is seeing smiling faces that are happy to taste freshly baked sweets made from scratch. In living my passion, I'm spiritually amped—ready and willing to dive into the satisfaction I get every day from baking."

To Brown, living a more modest life with purpose is more enriching than simply waiting to make partner or earning a six-figure paycheck. But making that kind of change takes great courage.

What are you passionately interested in? Why dismiss something you devote hours of your free time to as a silly obsession or hobby? If you're always rearranging friends' furniture and scouring flea markets for serendipitous treasures, maybe you have a natural talent for "staging" homes for sale. Sandi Genovese might never have become the queen of scrapbooking if she hadn't loved making a photo album of her family's trip to Hawaii so much twenty years ago. Scrapbooking was a pastime at first, but she quickly embraced it as a creative outlet, and from there she helped to tap into and fuel a national craze. Genovese is now a bestselling author and television host with her own line of paper-crafting products.

When you reorient your perspective to look for the magic in smaller, overlooked ideas, you may be surprised at what you discover—lucrative ideas that enrich not only your life but your bank account, too. "Find something you love to do," one saying has it, "and you'll never work another day in your life."

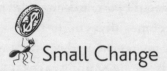

Small Change

SEE THE GLASS HALF EMPTY. Look around and see what's not working, what cries out for a solution. Take three items you use on a routine basis and ask yourself what small change would improve them.

BE FOUR AGAIN. Ask small questions. Don't be afraid to ask why, and, more importantly, why not. If you admire someone's success, be nosy about how he or she achieved it, instead of envious. Ask what specific steps they took and how they reached their goals.

TEST THE WATERS. If quilting is your passion and everyone raves about your work, maybe you shouldn't still be plodding along a career path you *don't* care about. Take a first baby step in another direction—rent a booth at a crafts show. At websites such as vocationvacations.com, you can even find brief internships in different businesses where you can test-drive your secret dream job.

MIX IT UP. Many great new entrepreneurial ideas are born from linking two disparate products together. Nike linked up with the Apple iPod so that while you're running, a wireless connection from your sneaker to your iPod nano tells you your mileage, time, distance, and pace and the calories you've burned. Think of completely different objects in your home or daily life. Is there a way to link them together? You might come up with the first shower that blows your hair dry as you towel off. When thinking big doesn't work, lower your sights—by thinking smaller.

Chapter 9
Small Changes the World

Remember there's no such thing as a small act of kindness. Every act creates a ripple with no logical end.
—Scott Adams

By following the tenets of thinking small, we believe, there is no limit to how great a difference we can make in the world. Too often we think that the global challenges we face today can only be solved by visionary leaders, unlimited resources, and international summits. Instead of looking to them to conquer the ills of the world—hunger, poverty, disease—why not look in the mirror instead?

Each and every one of us has the power to leave this world a better place than we found it. But we would argue that we do so not by creating grandiose plans, or imagining ourselves as some part of a vast movement, but by the small day-to-day actions and decisions that, together with the actions of millions of others, can transform the world.

Reinventing the Wheel(chair)

While vacationing in Morocco with his wife, Don Schoendorfer watched beggars jeer as a destitute, disabled woman dragged herself across the road by her fingernails. Watching this, Schoendorfer felt outraged, but powerless to help her. Nonetheless, the vision of this poor crippled woman scrabbling painfully across the Moroccan road stayed with him long after he returned to his comfortable home in Orange County, California.

In a world where astronauts rocket to the moon and four-year-olds cruise cul-de-sacs on motorized choo-choos, Schoendorfer believed that no one should have to suffer the indignity of immobility, whatever their infirmities. So he decided to start working on a solution himself. Schoendorfer, a mechanical engineer, spent the next several months scouring discount stores and tinkering through the night in his garage, determined to create a cheap, durable wheelchair that people in developing countries could afford and use.

The chair would have to be incredibly versatile, able to traverse mountains, negotiate swamps, and function in the heat and sands of the desert. It would have to withstand blistering heat and bitter cold. In most Third World countries, the world's poorest people couldn't dream of owning a standard wheelchair, much less one built for rugged terrain and climate. But Schoendorfer refused to give up. Finally, he was able to design an inexpensive chair that fit the bill: a plastic lawn chair mounted atop two mountain bike tires and a pair of cheap casters. Deceptively simple, but sturdy enough to withstand the elements. And the cost? Under fifty-two dollars.

One man's ingenuity and determination turned a ubiquitous piece of summer furniture—a cheap, seemingly indestructible plastic lawn chair—into a minor miracle for thousands of people around the world.

Today, Schoendorfer's nonprofit group, Free Wheelchair Mission, has delivered more than seventy-five thousand chairs to people in over thirty-three countries, including Angola, India, Peru, and Iraq. With more than 100 million disabled poor in developing countries, Schoendorfer says, "I have a small goal. Twenty million chairs given away free by 2010."

Schoendorfer's mission to help others, of course, is just a drop in the bucket in terms of the problems that need to be addressed. But he offers a path that others can follow. Peter Drucker, former president of the Rockefeller Foundation, sees a tremendous surge in what he refers to as the charitable "citizen sector"—hardworking people who are giving up a little of their free time to help others. They're not just holding bake sales to raise money for the local library. They're tackling the global problems of poverty, disease, and even warfare from their kitchen tables, without government funding, or contributions from businesses or major benefactors.

Groups of friends and volunteers are combining forces to create their own mini-philanthropies. That's the impetus behind social-giving circles, where individuals donate a small sum of money into a pooled fund and jointly decide how to give their collective grants or gifts away. Some groups ask members to pledge as little as a dollar a day, or to chip in thirty-five dollars at informal potlucks every few months. A dozen women in Washington, D.C., began a circle that eventually was able to give fifty thousand dollars to a psychologist to open a mental-health clinic in a troubled neighborhood. The number of giving circles has been mushrooming in recent years. Whether they're paying a utility bill to keep a needy family's power on in their community, or sending knitting machines to a women's collective in Rwanda, giving circles are having a measurable impact, having donated an estimated $100 million to date.

The nature of giving is shifting in the corporate world as well. Doing good and doing well are no longer contradictory goals. David Bornstein, author of *How to Change the World: Social Entrepreneurs and the Power of New Ideas,* claims that the citizen sector's zeal to fix a fractured world has given birth to hundreds of thousands of small new businesses, making social entrepreneurship "America's leading growth industry." Greg McHale, for example, a Boston computer geek and entrepreneur, designed a way for charities to hook up with volunteers in their own communities. Advertisers sponsor calendars of charitable events and requests for help, which are linked to articles on the local newspaper's Web page. The paper shares the ad revenue with McHale, who runs the good2gether.com site.

Einstein once mused that "our technology has exceeded our humanity." Today, technology is enabling us to reach humanitarian goals in ways that previously could not have been imagined. Now, with a search engine and the right spark of creativity, one lone person can help organize others to feed starving families halfway around the world—while helping the rest of us improve our vocabulary.

A Grain of an Idea

In October 2007, John Breen was sitting at his family's kitchen table in Bloomington, Indiana, using vocabulary flash cards to help his oldest son, Ben, study for the SAT. It was boring and repetitive, and every time Ben missed a word, his younger brother, Casey, taunted him. No one, except Casey, was having much fun, and the flash cards didn't seem to be helping Ben much. *There's got to be a better way,* thought his beleaguered father.

A computer programmer by trade, John Breen thought that a vocabulary computer game might be a way to capture his son's attention, and boost his SAT scores. At the same time, Breen had been working on designing a website to help his favorite cause—ending world hunger. "It's a pretty easy thing to fix," he believes. "It's very doable. It's not like curing cancer, where you have to have a big breakthrough—just people having the will to end it."

So he decided to try combining his two projects and, in the process, cooked up FreeRice.com. Breen spent an entire summer programming thousands of words and their definitions into his new game. Every time you click on the correct definition for a word, a donation of twenty grains of rice is made to the UN World Food Programme. The United Nations provides worldwide distribution of the rice, which is paid for by the advertisers on the site, who are ebullient (Definition: "happy," add twenty grains) about being associated with its propitious (Definition: "favorable," add twenty grains) results.

Since its inception, FreeRice has attracted millions of

players and averages forty thousand people—and 150 million grains of rice—daily. It has generated donations totaling 42 billion grains of rice. While an individual player's donation of three hundred, five hundred, or even a thousand grains might not seem like much, says WFP spokeswoman Jennifer Parmelee, "each player is making a difference as part of a huge collective effort."

"It's not what I did," Breen told us. "It's about all the people who take a leap of faith that if we all do a little bit, combined, it will be a big bit."

In colleges and universities around the country, more and more students are hungering for careers that will help those in need. Among those leading the way is the Colin Powell Center for Policy Studies at the City College of New York. The center has begun sponsoring the Service-Learning Faculty Fellowship Program, which provides support for courses geared toward service careers in education, health, and community outreach.

The results of these individual efforts are inspiring. Investing in the power and passion of youth is always worthwhile. In fact, we have found that many of the biggest hearts are beating in the smallest chests.

No One Is Too Small

When twelve-year-old Craig Kielburger was searching for the comics in the newspaper, he came across an article about a Pakistani boy who had been sold into slavery as a carpet weaver at the age of four, and then was murdered at age twelve for speaking out against the injustices of child labor. The realization that a boy his own age had died trying to help others shocked Craig. As he read on, he learned that over a quarter of a billion children in the world are forced to work every day. Those children don't know what it is like to go to school every morning, or play ball on a sunny afternoon, or simply to come home and know that dinner will be on the table. Craig couldn't stop thinking about the murdered Pakistani boy, and the one small voice against injustice that had been silenced. Craig invited ten classmates over for pizza to think of a way to help. The outraged youngsters decided to raise their voices, to make that one child's lost cry the shout of thousands. The result was an organization called Free the Children, whose mission is to stop the exploitation of children and, as Craig told interviewers, "to free children from the idea that we were powerless and could not change the world." Today, Craig is twenty-three, and Free the Children, working with partners like the United Nations, is the largest organization of children helping children in the world.

Shauna Fleming is another youngster who was not willing to turn away. As a high school freshman, Shauna was watching the news one night when she caught a report about American soldiers overseas feeling unappreciated by the people back home. She needed to fulfill a community service credit at school, and the news report gave her an idea.

"Dad," announced Shauna to her father, who was paying bills in the next room, "I'm going to send thank-you notes to the troops."

"Great," he replied absently.

"How many do you think I'll need?"

"A million," he told her.

Shauna took him at his word, and proceeded to call, write, and e-mail everyone she knew about writing to the American troops, and they each called a friend themselves, and so on and so on. Her father sent out press releases for her, and their local paper called for an interview. Then Shauna got a call from the Associated Press, which put her story out on the wire to newspapers around the world. Soon, Shauna was setting her alarm for 3:30 a.m. to do morning talk-show interviews on the East Coast. Boxes and boxes of letters arrived at her school, where an empty classroom was needed to store them until Shauna could get them shipped overseas, with the help of classmates who gave up their free time for sorting parties. "It just started to snowball," Shauna recalls. She met her goal within six months, and was invited to deliver the millionth letter in person to President Bush in the Oval Office.

Four years later, Shauna is in college and has written a book about her experience. Her organization, A Million Thanks, has two hundred chapters around the country. The number of letters has risen to four million, and they are still coming.

"If I touched even one person's life, it's all worth it," she says.

There's a Hero in Each of Us

There is probably no organization better founded on the power of small than the Make-A-Wish Foundation. Their mantra is simple: there are thousands of critically ill children in America, and each one of them has a wish. And every one of us has the power to help it come true. When our agency was asked to come up with an advertising campaign to promote the organization's efforts, creative directors John Murphy and Simon Hunt, with the generous donated help of a director, composer, and production crews, re-created the wish of one very special little boy: Michael Lucco.

Michael Lucco was six years old, struggling with cystic fibrosis. Michael's health problems were considerable: He was in and out of hospitals, often too sick to go to school. But what he yearned to do most, he told his parents, was to help others. And in a little boy's imagination, that meant just one thing: Becoming a superhero.

The Make-A-Wish people went to work creating Michael's chosen alter ego—Beetleboy, sidekick to Michael's all-time superhero, Spider-Man.

A young girl offered to design Beetleboy's sunshine yellow costume with one red glove and one green. Her mother did the sewing. Stu Snodgrass, a young member of the Make-A-Wish staff, agreed to don a leotard and run through town as the villainous Green Goblin. A local TV anchor taped a fake news broadcast with an appeal for Beetleboy's help. The Pittsburgh Zoo, the University of Pittsburgh, and even the mayor's office and sheriff all agreed to play along.

On the appointed morning, Michael looked up from his breakfast in dismay when his usual cartoons were interrupted by an urgent news bulletin. The city was in peril!

"Beetleboy," the anchor implored, "if you can hear me, we need your help!"

His father, Greg Lucco, will never forget how Michael leapt up from the table, pulled on his costume, and dashed out the front door. Waiting in the driveway was a shiny red Volkswagen Beetle, loaned by a local car dealership. A sheriff's escort was also waiting. First stop was the Pittsburgh Zoo, where Michael held up a red glove to stop the kiddie train from running over a beautiful damsel tied to the tracks. The Green Goblin got away, however, and Beetleboy chased him to the university, where the Goblin was threatening to launch "poisonous footballs" at the Pittsburgh Panther mascot. Throngs of university employees, alerted by e-mail, filled the stands to cheer on Beetleboy as he thwarted the villain once again. The school's marching band spilled onto the field to pay musical tribute to Beetleboy, and the football coach came out to personally thank him. Michael beamed, until the JumboTron flashed another threat from the Green Goblin, who was going to poison the town's water supply.

At a nearby state park, Beetleboy spotted the Goblin running away from one of the city's most beloved fountains, which was dry. As he raised his green glove, a hidden waterworks employee made the water shoot up again at his command.

Finally, after one last chase through the streets of Pittsburgh—to the applause of dozens of passersby—Beetleboy cornered his nemesis on the steps of city hall, where the Green Goblin was waiting with a box of dynamite. With the help of his dad and some sheriff's deputies,

Beetleboy threw a huge net over the villain and watched in satisfaction as the handcuffs were snapped on. Out came the mayor and county sheriff to personally thank Beetleboy and swear him in as the city's official superhero.

And then came the crowning touch: a congratulatory visit by Spider-Man himself, sent from New York by Marvel Comics.

In all, Make-A-Wish officials figure some five hundred people participated, in one way or another, in making Michael's wish come true.

Now in high school, Michael still vividly remembers that magical day. His favorite part? "I really, really enjoyed the thrill of actually helping people and making a difference."

● ● ●

When we started The Kaplan Thaler Group, we set out to make a difference in the way that we ran a company. We didn't have a brilliant game plan, or a bottomless bank account, or even a long list of clients. We had a single account, a cramped home office, and the kind of tunnel vision that turned out to be our greatest asset. We built our business—and our reputations—day by day, brick by brick, idea by idea. We simply knew no other way and had no other options.

But once we saw the power it had, small became the vital element of our professional and personal lives, nurturing both our careers and our relationships. Focusing on the tiniest details of the work we love, finding magic in even the smallest inspirations, embracing the briefest moments—that's where the passion is.

So what about you? Why not embrace the power of small in your life? There's a world that needs fixing, a career waiting to soar, a life ready to be transformed into the extraordinary.

Take the first small step.

And then keep on walking.

Index

. . .

accountability, 106–7
Adams, Scott, 122
Aflac, 35–36, 52, 85
Alba-Lim, Michelle, 53–55
Amico, Tom, 36
A Million Thanks, 128–29
Anderson, Sandie, 31–33
Animated Storyboard, 13
Apple iPod, 121
appreciation, 22, 36–38, 45, 55, 62
attention, pay a little more, 50–52
Attention-Deficit Trait (ADT), 51–52
Ausnes, Annamarie, 31–33

Bale, Elvin, 88–90
Bare Escentuals, 111–12
Beers, Charlotte, 82
behavior modification, 68
Berra, Yogi, 85
Blodgett, Leslie, 111–12
body clock, 69
body language, 17, 27, 81–82, 86, 87
Boren, Molly, 60–61, 69
Bornstein, David, 125

brain physiology, 63–64, 76, 78
Brant, Paul, 66
Breen, John, 126–27
Broken Windows, Broken Business (Levine), 95
Brown, Warren, 117–19
Bryan, William Jennings, 56
Buber, Martin, 51
business
    appreciate the staff, 36–37, 45, 54
    attention to detail, 4, 15, 21, 55, 90–92, 93, 106
    cues and clues, *73–74, 77,* 81, 83–85, 86
    conversation before meetings, 29–30, 35–36, 38
    conversation skills, 34
    creativity, 108–11, 114–16
    do what you love, 110, 117–20
    employee suggestions, 18–20
    esprit de corps, 8, 45
    fill a need, 116–17
    hiring, 97–99
    honesty about lack of knowledge, 99–102

job interviews, 16–17, 41–45
make it big by thinking
    small, 108–21
niche markets, 111–13
presentation rehearsals,
    104–5
use of time zones, 13
Butler Bag, 114

CakeLove, 119
California Prune Board,
    113–14
Carducci, Bernardo, 27
career, 1–3, 117–20, 127
charity activities, 5–7, 122–32
children changing the world,
    127–29
Clairol, 15–16, 46
Clarke, Jamie, 4, 105–6
Claxton, Guy, 76
Clinton, Pres. Bill, 83
communication. *See also* e-mail
    attention to the other person,
        37–38, 39, 83, 86
    body language, 17, 27,
        81–82, 86, 87
    child development, 30–31
    conversation skills, 34
    courteous encounters,
        24–26, 28–29, 31–33,
        38–39
    cues and clues, 80–83, 86–87
    embrace "stranger danger,"
        38–39
    finding common ground,
        28–30

first impressions, 34, 44–45
foreign language, 95
with kids while driving, 40
play reporter, 39
"please" and "thank you,"
    36–37, 47–49
starved for conversation,
    26–28
telephone, 51
written, 47–48, 55, 93–94
Continental Airlines, 46–47
Crocs, 113
cues and clues, 71–87

Dalai Lama, 88
David, Eric, 35–36
Davis, Edward, 79
details, attention to
    to avoid mistakes, 88–95,
        105–6
    cheat sheet, 106
    to create impression, 4, 15,
        21, 48–49, 50, 55, 91
    practice and fine tuning,
        104–6
Dickinson, Emily, 12
Dog Poop Girl, 14
Drucker, Peter, 124
Dweck, Carol, 67, 102–3

Ebbesmeyer, Curtis, 72–73
effort, go the extra inch,
    41–55
Einstein, Albert, 125
El Cortez Hotel, 19–20
Ellet, Charles, Jr., 56–57

e-mail, 4, 13, 26–27, 39, 52, 81
exercise, 64–65, 66

Fangio, Juan, 74–75
Fimple, Scott, 20–21
Fleming, Shauna, 128–29
focus, stay in the moment,
    103–5
Ford, 95
FreeRice.com, 126–27
Free the Children, 128
Free Wheelchair Mission, 124
Fripp, Patricia, 1–2

Gardner, Carol, 108–11
Genovese, Sandi, 119
gifts, receiving, 48
Girl Scouts, 9–10
global effects of individual
    actions, 122–33
goals
  break down into small tasks,
    22, 57–70
  career, 1–3, 119–20
  kaizen approach, 62–64
  motivation to begin, 59, 61,
    63
  problem-solving, 57–60,
    62–64, 102, 115–16
Goleman, Daniel, 30, 51
Goman, Carol Kinsey, 34
good2gether.com, 125
Greenwald, Rachel, 82–83
Griffith, Adm. Dwayne, 21
Groover, Jen, 114
Gumbiner, Paul, 44–45

Hallmark, 110
Hallowell, Edward, 51
Hammarskjöld, Dag, 71
*Hare Brain, Tortoise Mind: Why
    Intelligence Increases When
    You Think Less* (Claxton),
    76
Harrell, Dr. Thomas, 34
Hay, Kathleen, 100–101
home organization, 60–62,
    69–70
*How to Change the World: Social
    Entrepreneurs and the Power
    of New Ideas* (Bornstein),
    125
How to Solve It (Pólya), 59
Hsieh, Tony, 98
Huggin, Ambros, 115
humor, 35–36, 97
Hunt, Simon, 130

ideas
  creativity, 63–64, 108–11,
    114–16, 120–21
  reinvention, 117
  use in another context,
    71–73, 77
  use of two disparate, 120–21
"I–It" interaction, 50–51
impressions
  first, 34, 44–45
  impact of small, 11, 20–21,
    23
information overload, 4,
    12–15, 48, 50–52, 73
Ingraham, James, 72–73

initiative, taking the, 41–45
InnoCentive, 115
Internet
  it's a byte-sized world,
    12–15, 51
  level playing field, 115
  limitations of communication
    via, 26–27, 81
  privacy issues, 13–14
intuition and instincts, 17, 54,
    74–80, 98–99

jet lag, 69
Jibbitz, 113

kaizen approach, 62–64
Kashdan, Todd, 38
Kielburger, Craig, 127–28
kindness
  to create opportunities, 21
  impact on relationships, 4,
    5–7, 16, 55
  impressions made by, 11,
    20–21, 23
  random acts of, 53–54
KISS, 98
Kissinger, Henry, 86
Knowles, Edmond, 66
Kodak, 78
Koval, Kenny, 41–44
Kraft, 10
Krausz, Ezra, 13

Lefton, Dr. Lester, 27, 44, 82
Leno, Jay, 37
LePore, Theresa, 18

Levine, Michael, 94–95
*Lifetime of Observations and
    Reflections On and Off the
    Court, A* (Wooden), 7
list, action, 22
love, do what you, 117–20
Lucco, Michael, 130–32

Make-A-Wish Foundation,
    129–32
Markman, Howard, 6
Maurer, Dr. Robert, 63
McHale, Greg, 125
Meyer, Danny, 48–49, 77
microbehaviors, 79–80
Miller, Charles, III, 79
*Mindset: The New Psychology
    of Success* (Dweck),
    102
mini-tasking, 22
mistakes, effects of small,
    88–107
  ability to laugh at yourself,
    96–97
  asking questions, 101–2
  attention to detail, 88–93
  double-checking to avoid,
    93–95
  with foreign languages, 95
  practice and fine tuning,
    104–5
  stay in the moment, 103
money, 66–67, 69, 125–26
Morgan, Dr. Bill, 64
MTV, 47
Murphy, John, 130

Niagara Falls Suspension Bridge, 56–58
Nike, 120–21
Nonverbal Advantage, The (Goman), 34

O'Donnell, Rosie, 47
"one day at a time," twelve-step programs' mantra, 62
One Small Step Can Change Your Life: The Kaizen Way (Maurer), 63
opportunities, small, 21, 53–55
Outback Restaurants, 60

parenting, 9–10, 26, 40, 67
Parker Pen, 95
passion, 117–20
perception
  of others, 27, 33, 34
  of self, 1–3, 9–10
Pinizzotto, Anthony, 78–79
"please" and "thank you," 36–37, 47–49
Pólya, George, 58–59
Powell, Gen. Colin, 49, 50
praise, 37, 67–68, 82
presidential election of 2000, 17–18
privacy issues, 13–14
protoconversations, 30–31
Proust, Marcel, 108

questions, asking, 101–2, 120

Radcliffe, Paula, 64–65
relationships
  behavior modification, 68
  dating, 82–83
  impact of small actions, 5–7, 8–9, 17
  impact of small impressions, 11, 20–21, 23
  subtle cues, 9–10, 17, 74
  we cannot change others, 6
Revlon, 104
rewards, 64–65
Robert, Chris, 35
Robert Solomon and Associates, 99–102
Roberts, Chief Justice John, 97
Rose, Paul, 38
Roster, Catherine, 47–48

Sadove, Steve, 15–16, 46
Schmelzer, Sheri, 113
Schoendorfer, Don, 122–24
Sears, 82
senses, five, 78–80
Simmons, Gene, 98
Simplicity Works Organizing Services, 60–61
Snodgrass, Stu, 130
sports, 64–65, 74–76, 85, 103, 105–6
Starbucks Rule, 44–45
success, mindset for, 102–3
Sullivan & Cromwell, 36–37
Sutherland, Amy, 67–68

Tallerico, Randall, 99–102
Teresa, Mother, 1
Terkel, Studs, 26
Toyota, 63
Toys "R" Us, 10, 90–92
truths, small, 12–23
  appreciation, 22, 36–38, 45,
    55, 62
  everyone matters, 17–20
  impressions, 11, 20–21, 23,
    34, 44
  it's a byte-size world, 12–15
  a little good goes a long way,
    20–21
  mini-tasking, 22, 57–70
  small acts tell a larger story,
    4, 15–17
Twain, Mark, 24

Union Square Café, 48–49
United Nations, 126–27,
  128

Wal-Mart, 54
Walsh, Homan, 58
Walton, Sam, 54
weight loss, 65–66
*What Shamu Taught Me About
  Life, Love, and Marriage*
  (Sutherland), 68
Why He Didn't Call You Back
  (Greenwald), 82–83
Wizmark, 112
WLF Interactive Development
  Centre, 53–55
women, fear of math and
  science, 9–10
Wooden, John, 7
Wright, Kendal, 92

Zagat, Tim and Nina,
  116–17
Zagat Guides, 117
Zappos, 97–98
Zelda Wisdom, 108–11